These are the words of fifteen-year-old Daisy Bates, who, one morning in 1962, set out to enter a public high school in Little Rock, Arkansas:

"*Somebody started yelling, 'Lynch her!' 'Lynch her!' I tried to see a friendly face somewhere in the mob—someone who maybe would help. I looked into the face of an old woman and it seemed a kind face, but when I looked at her again, she spat on me.*"

In White America is a dramatization of an ordeal that profanes humanity. Using the actual testimony of whites and Negroes as recorded in speeches, diaries, letters, and other historical documents, Martin B. Duberman tells the story of the two-centuries-long struggle of the American Negro for freedom. His play is unusual and revealing. Nothing quite like it has ever before been presented in the American theater.

"It is true and overwhelmingly important. . . . It is theatre . . . in the best sense: moving, funny, humane, genuine, and, best of all, unflaggingly provocative."
— John Simon, *The Hudson Review*

This Signet edition includes an appendix of supporting documents, notes on the documents on which the drama is based, and the author's brilliant essay on the role of history in the dramatic arts.

SIGNET Books of Special Interest

IN
WHITE AMERICA

A Documentary Play
by MARTIN DUBERMAN

With an Afterword by the Author

A SIGNET BOOK
Published by THE NEW AMERICAN LIBRARY

SIGNET TRADEMARK REG. U.S. PAT. OFF. AND FOREIGN COUNTRIES
REGISTERED TRADEMARK—MARCA REGISTRADA
HECHO EN CHICAGO, U.S.A.

SIGNET BOOKS are published by
The New American Library, Inc.,
1301 Avenue of the Americas, New York, New York 10019

FIRST PRINTING, AUGUST, 1965

PRINTED IN THE UNITED STATES OF AMERICA

For Lu and Irv
with love

ACKNOWLEDGMENTS

I owe a great debt to the producer, Judith Rutherford Marechal, to the director, Harold Stone, and to the cast, who brought this script to life in its original production. I am grateful for their fine talents, and also for the deep pleasure of working with them.

There are three other people I wish to thank: Robert F. Engs, for a large variety of assists; my sister, Lucile Milberg, who sat with me on the rocks at a critical point; and Claire Degener Lord, who invented me as a playwright.

M.B.D.

PREFACE

PLAYS do not usually require prefaces—unless, like Mr. Shaw, we are not yet certain if the point has been won. The reason for this note is less combative: I would like to explain why I tried to make a "play" out of historical documents.

My starting point was the wish to describe what it has been like to be a Negro in this country (to the extent that a white man can describe it). Neither popular journalism nor professional history has made much effort to tell this story. Both have been dominated by whites, and the whites, whether from guilt, indifference, or hostility, have been slow to reveal the American Negro's past. The revelations are painful, but they must be faced if the present is to be understood, and the future made more tolerable.

Negroes are themselves often unfamiliar with their history. The truth has not been easy to come by in a society dominated by whites, nor easy to digest; old wounds, old degradations, must in the name of self-respect be avoided. Yet if there is much in this history to enrage or sadden the Negro, there is also much to make him proud: here is a people who maintained their humanity while being treated inhumanly, who managed to endure as men while being defined as property.

I chose to tell this story on the stage, and through historical documents, because I wanted to combine the evocative power of the spoken word with the confirming power of historical fact. The spoken word is able to call forth the binding emotions of pity and sympathy. Men would feel, not merely understand, the Negro's story. His experience might thereby become our own, past reality might enter into present consciousness. The resulting compassion would be further validated by the documentary format. Americans, admirers of "fact," would have difficulty discounting their concern if based solidly on the "stuff" of history.

It was easier to formulate these goals than to find the materials to meet them. To some extent professional history, which aims at the comprehensive, and professional theater, which relies on the selective, are at cross-purposes. Yet a "documentary play" on the Negro, to deserve that title, must somehow be both good history and good theater, must try to be a genuinely representative sample of Negro life and at the same time a vivid and moving one. This best of all possible worlds can only be approximated. How close I have come, I cannot say. I have gone through hundreds of sources and thousands of notes, but diligence and good intentions, however much they may solace the Puritan heart, have never yet guaranteed success. All I am sure of is that the documentary technique in the theater is worth exploring, and, even more, that the story of being black "in white America" desperately needs telling.

MARTIN B. DUBERMAN

January 12, 1964
Princeton University

CONTENTS

In White America was first presented at the Sheridan Square Playhouse, New York City, on October 31, 1963

ORIGINAL CAST

Gloria Foster   Claudette Nevins
James Greene   Michael O'Sullivan
Moses Gunn   Fred Pinkard

Produced by Judith Rutherford Marechal
Directed by Harold Stone
Designed by Robin Wagner
Music performed by Billy Faier

A NOTE ON THE TEXT

Except for introductory narratives, the material is presented as originally written or spoken. None of the documents, of course, has been used in its entirety, but in editing I have not added or paraphrased except in those very few cases where a word or two was absolutely necessary for clarity or transition.

I have left the text "clean" rather than clutter it with endless diacritical marks to denote omitted material or minor changes. However, to give a sample of the editorial technique used, I have printed four of the complete documents in an Appendix, and have marked those portions excerpted for the script, as well as any insertions made. Ideally, the Appendix would contain all the original documents, but this was not possible, since many of the selections in the script are drawn from scattered sections of large books.

In "Notes on the Documents," I have listed the original sources, and discussed, wherever applicable, any small changes which I have made in them.

The songs in this script are suggestions only; they are those used in the original production.

Act 1

ACT 1

(On stage: 3 Negro and 3 white actors, 2 men and 1 woman in each case, and a guitarist)

(WHITE MAN comes forward, picks newspaper off table and reads aloud from it the current date.)

WHITE MAN:
[January 12, 1964]
If God had intended for the races to mix, he would have mixed them himself. He put each color in a different place.

NEGRO MAN:
The American white man has a conscience, and the nonviolent method appeals to that conscience.

WHITE WOMAN:
Negroes are demanding something that isn't so unreasonable—to get a cup of coffee at a lunch counter, to get a decent job.

NEGRO WOMAN:
What they really feel on the inside never changes. Eventually they'll wind up calling you a nigger.

WHITE MAN:

Negro impatience can be readily understood, but defiance breeds doubt, and riots breed hatred.

NEGRO MAN:

Sure I love my white brother, but I watch him!

NEGRO MAN:

To integrate with evil is to be destroyed with evil. We want an area of this land we can call our own.

WHITE WOMAN:

My children won't be taking sides—unless we idiots tell them there are sides to take.

NEGRO MAN:

After 400 years of barbaric treatment, the American Negro is fed up with the unmitigated hypocrisy of the white man.

WHITE MAN (*reading again from newspaper*):

If they got guts enough to come down here all they'll get is a load of buckshot. The white people have shown remarkable restraint in not killing niggers wholesale. [January 12, 1964]

NEGRO ACTRESS (*sings*):
Oh, freedom, Oh, freedom,
Oh, freedom, over me!
And before I'll be a slave,
I'll be buried in my grave,
And go home to my Lord
And be free.

NARRATOR:

(*Throughout the play the delivery of the narratives is alternated among the actors.*)

The story of the Negro in the United States begins with

the slave trade. A ship's doctor aboard a slave vessel in the mid-eighteenth century, described his impressions.

SHIP DOCTOR

The slave ships lie a mile below the town, in Bonny River, off the coast of Guinea. Sometimes fifteen sail meet here together. Scarce a day passes without some negroes being purchased and carried on board . . .

The wretched negroes are immediately fastened together, two and two, by handcuffs on their wrists and by irons rivetted on their legs. They are then sent down between the decks and placed in a space partitioned off for that purpose. They are frequently stowed so close as to admit of no other position than lying on their sides. Nor will the height between decks allow them to stand.

The diet of the negroes while on board, consists chiefly of horsebeans boiled to the consistence of a pulp.

Upon the negroes refusing to take food, I have seen coals of fire, glowing hot, put on a shovel and placed so near their lips as to scorch and burn them. I have also been credibly informed that a certain captain in the slave-trade, poured melted lead on such of his negroes as obstinately refused their food.

On board some ships the common sailors are allowed to have intercourse with such of the black women whose consent they can procure. The officers are permitted to indulge their passions among them at pleasure.

The hardships suffered by the negroes during the passage are scarcely to be conceived. The exclusion of fresh air is the most intolerable. Whenever the sea is rough and the rain heavy it becomes necessary to shut every conveyance by which air is admitted. The negroes' rooms very soon grow intolerably hot. The confined air produces fevers and fluxes which carry off great numbers of them. The floor of their rooms can be so covered with blood and mucus in consequence of the flux, that it resembles a slaughter-house. Last week by only continuing among them for about a quarter of an hour, I was so overcome with the heat, stench, and foul air that I nearly fainted; and it was only with assistance that I could get on deck . . .

One evening while the ship lay in Bonny River, one of the negroes forced his way through the network on the larboard side of the vessel, jumped overboard and was devoured by the sharks. Circumstances of this kind are very frequent.

Very few of the negroes can bear the loss of their liberty and the hardships they endure.

> NEGRO ACTRESS (*sings*):
> *And before I'll be a slave,*
> *I'll be buried in my grave,*
> *And go home to my Lord*
> *And be free.*

QUAKER WOMAN (*reads aloud from parchment*):
February 11, 1790. To the Senate and House of Representatives of the United States: The Address of the people called Quakers, in their annual assembly convened.

Firmly believing that unfeigned righteousness in public as well as private stations, is the only sure ground of hope for the Divine blessing, we apprehend ourselves religiously bound to request your serious christian attention, to the gross national iniquity of trafficking in the persons of fellow-men.

Many are the enormities abhorrent to common humanity, and common honesty, which we judge it not needful to particularise to a body of men, chosen as eminently distinguished for wisdom as extensive information. But we find it indispensably incumbent on us, to attempt to excite your attention to the affecting subject, that a sincere and impartial inquiry may take place, whether it be not in reality within your power to exercise justice and mercy, which, if adhered to, we cannot doubt, must produce the abolition of the slave trade.

FIRST CONGRESSMAN:

Mr. President, this petition prays that we should take measures for the abolition of the slave trade. This is desiring an unconstitutional act, because the Constitution secures that trade to the States, independent of Congressional restrictions, for a term of twenty-one years. Therefore, it ought to be rejected as an attempt upon the virtue and patriotism of the House.

SECOND CONGRESSMAN:

I think it is incumbent upon every member of this House to sift the subject well, and ascertain what can be done to restrain a practice so nefarious. The Constitution has authorized us to levy a tax upon the importation of such persons. I would willingly go to that extent; and if anything further can be devised to discountenance the trade, consistent with the terms of the Constitution, I shall cheerfully give it my assent and support.

FIRST CONGRESSMAN:

I fear that if Congress takes any measures indicative of an intention to interfere with the kind of property alluded to, it would sink in value very considerably, and might be injurious to a great number of citizens, particularly in the Southern States.

SECOND CONGRESSMAN:

I think the gentleman carries his apprehensions too far. It appears to me, that if the importation was crushed, the value of a slave would be increased instead of diminished.

FIRST CONGRESSMAN:

I differ much in opinion. If through the interference of the General Government the slave trade was abolished, it would evince to the people a disposition towards a total emancipation, and they would hold their property in jeopardy. The petitioners may as well come forward and solicit Congress to interdict the West India trade, because from thence we import rum, which has a debasing influence upon the consumer. But, sir, is the whole morality of the United States confined to the Quakers? Do they understand the rights of mankind, and the disposition of Providence, better than others? If they were to consult that Book, which claims our regard, they will find that slavery is not only allowed but commended. And if they fully examine the subject, they will find that slavery has been no novel doctrine since the days of Cain; but be these things as they may, I hope the House will order the petition to lie on the table, in order to prevent alarm to our Southern brethren.

NARRATOR:

The Quaker petition on the slave trade was tabled. Yet the whole question of the Negro's place in American life continued to disturb a few thoughtful men. Among them was Thomas Jefferson.

JEFFERSON:

The love of justice and the love of country plead equally the cause of these people, and it is a moral reproach to us that they should have pleaded it so long in vain. Yet the hour of emancipation is advancing. Nothing is more certainly written in the book of fate, than that these people are to be free; nor is it less certain that the two races, equally free, cannot live in the same government. Nature, habit, opinion, have drawn indelible lines of distinction between them.

(*Coming forward*)

The blacks are at least as brave, and more adventuresome. But this may perhaps proceed from a want of forethought, which prevents their seeing a danger till it be present. They are more ardent after their female; but love seems with them to be more an eager desire, than a tender delicate mixture of sentiment and sensation. Their griefs are transient. Those numberless afflictions, which render it doubtful whether heaven has given life to us in mercy or in wrath, are less felt, and sooner forgotten with them. In general, their existence appears to participate more of sensation than reflection. It appears to me that in memory they are equal to the whites; in reason much inferior, as I think one could scarcely be found capable of tracing and comprehending the investigations of Euclid. It will be right to make great allowances for the difference of condition, of education, of conversation, of the sphere in which they move. Yet we know that among the Romans, the condition of their slaves was much more deplorable than that of the blacks on the continent of America. Notwithstanding, their slaves were often their rarest artists. They excelled too in science . . . But they were of the race of whites.

To justify a general conclusion, requires many observations. I advance it, therefore, as a suspicion only, that the blacks, whether originally a distinct race, or made distinct by time and circumstances, are inferior to the whites in the endowments both of body and mind.

NEGRO ACTOR (*sings*):
My old missus promised me,
Hmm-mm-mm,
When she die, gonna set me free,
Hm-mm-mm.

Missus die nine years ago,
Hmm-mm-mm,
Here ah is in the same old row,
Hm-mm-mm.

NARRATOR:
White men rarely heard the slaves themselves talk about their condition. One of the few exceptions was a conversation recorded by a Northern journalist, Frederick Law Olmsted, with a house servant named William.

OLMSTED (*to audience*):

After leaving a plantation near New Orleans, I was driven about twenty miles in a buggy, by one of the house servants. He was inclined to be talkative and as he expressed great affection and respect for his owner, I felt at liberty to question him on some points upon which I had always previously avoided conversing with slaves. (*Crossing to where the slave, William, is seated*) He first said that he came from Virginia . . .

WILLIAM:

I reckon there is no black folks anywhere so well made as those who was born in Virginny. Is you from New Orleans, massa?

OLMSTED:

No, I live in the North.

WILLIAM:

Da's great many brack folks dah, massa?

OLMSTED:

No; very few.

WILLIAM:

Da's a great many in Virginny.

OLMSTED:

But I came from beyond Virginia—from New York.

WILLIAM:

If I was free, I would go to Virginny, and see my old mudder. I don't well know, exactly, how old I is; but I rec'lect, de day I was taken away, my ole mudder she tell me I was tirteen years old. I felt dreadful bad, but now I like it here. De people is almost all French. Is dere any French in New York?

OLMSTED:

Yes, but not as many as in Louisiana.

WILLIAM:

I s'pose dah is more of French people in Lusiana den dah is anywhar else in all de world—a'nt, dah, massa?

OLMSTED:

Except in France.

WILLIAM:

Wa's dat, sar?

OLMSTED:

France is the country where all the Frenchmen came from, in the first place.

WILLIAM:

Wa's dat France, massa?

OLMSTED:

France is a country across the ocean, the big water, beyond Virginia, where all the Frenchmen first came from; just as the black people all came first from Africa, you know.

WILLIAM:

Is de brack folks better off to be here, massa?

OLMSTED:

I think so.

WILLIAM:

Why is it, then, massa, when de brack people is free, dey wants to send 'em away out of dis country?

OLMSTED (*taken aback*):

Some people think Africa is a better place for you. (*Changing the subject*) What would you do, if you were free?

WILLIAM:

If I was free, massa; *if I was free* . . . I would—Well, sar, de fus thing I would do, if I was free, I would go to work for a year, and get some money for myself,—den-den-den-den, massa, dis is what I do—I buy me, fus place, a little house, and little lot land, and den-no; den-den- I would go to old Virginny, and see my old mudder. Yes, sar, I would like to do dat fus thing; den, when I com back, de fus thing I'd do, I'd get me a wife; den, I'd take her to my house, and I would live with her dar; and I would raise things in my garden, and take 'em to New Orleans, and sell 'em dar, in the market. Dat's de way I would live, if I was free.

OLMSTED:

Well, now, wouldn't you rather live on a plantation with a kindly master like yours than to be free, William?

WILLIAM:

Oh! no, sir, I'd rather be free! Oh, yes, sir, I'd like it better to be free; I would dat, master.

OLMSTED:

Why would you?

WILLIAM:

Why, you see, master, if I was free—if I was *free,* I'd have all my time to myself. I'd rather work for myself. Yes. I'd like dat better.

OLMSTED:

But then, you know, you'd have to take care of yourself, and you'd get poor.

WILLIAM:

No, sir, I would not get poor, I would get rich; for you see, master, then I'd work all the time for myself.

OLMSTED:

You don't suppose there would be much sugar raised, do you?

WILLIAM:

Why, yes, master, I do. Why not, sir? What would de brack people do? Wouldn't dey hab to work for dar libben? and de wite people own all de land—war dey goin' to work? Dey hire demself right out again, and work harder dan dey do now to get more wages—a heap harder. I tink so, sir. I would do so, sir.

OLMSTED:

The black people talk among themselves about this, do they; and they think so generally?

WILLIAM:

Oh! yes, sir; dey talk so; dat's wat dey tink.

OLMSTED:

Then they talk about being free a good deal, do they?

WILLIAM:

Yes, sir. Dey—(*suddenly on guard*) dat is, dey say dey wish it was so; dat's all dey talk, master—dat's all, sir.
(*The light fades.*)

NARRATOR:

Some of William's fellow slaves were interviewed many years later about their recollections of slavery.

MAN:

I sets and 'members the times in the world. I 'members now clear as yesterday things I forgot for a long time. I 'members 'bout the days of slavery, and I don't 'lieve they ever gwine have slaves no more on this earth. I think God done took that burden offen his black children, and I'm aiming to praise Him for it to His face in the days of glory.

WOMAN:

I's hear tell of them good slave days, but I ain't never seen no good times then. One time Aunt Cheyney was just out of bed with a suckling baby and she run away. Old Solomon gits the nigger hounds and takes her trail. They gits near her and she grabs a limb and tries to hist herself in a tree, but them dogs grap her and pull her down. The men hollers them onto her, and the dogs tore her naked and et the breasts plumb off her body. She got well and lived to be a old woman, but 'nother woman has to suck her baby, and she ain't got no sign of breasts no more.

MAN:

Sometimes I wishes that I could be back to the old place, 'cause we did have plenty to eat, and at hog-killing time us had more'n a plenty. Old Master kill eight or ten set-down hogs at one time . . . What a set-down hog? It's a hog what done et so much corn he got so fat that he feets can't hold him up, and he just set on he hind quarters and grunts and eats, and eats and grunts, till they knock him in the head.

MAN:

Talking 'bout victuals, our eating was good. Can't say the same for all places. Some of the plantations half-starved their niggers till they wasn't fitting for work. They had to slip about to other places to piece out their meals.

WOMAN:

I recollects once when I was trying to clean the house like Ole Miss tell me, I finds a biscuit, and I's so hungry I et it, 'cause we never see such a thing as a biscuit . . . and she comes in and say, "Where that biscuit?" I say, "Miss, I et it 'cause I's so hungry." Then she grabs that broom and start to beating me over the head with it and calling me low-down nigger, and I guess I just clean lost my head 'cause I knowed better than to fight her if I knowed anything 't all, but I start to fight her, and the driver, he comes in and he grabs me and starts beating me with that cat-o'-nine-tails, and he beats me till I fall to the floor nearly dead. He cut my back all to pieces, then they rubs salt in the cuts for more punishment. Lord, Lord, honey! Them was awful days.

MAN:

The niggers didn't go to the church building; the preacher came and preached to them in their quarters. He'd just say, "Serve your masters. Don't steal your master's turkey. Don't steal your master's chickens. Don't steal your master's hogs. Don't steal your master's meat. Do whatsomever your master tells you to do." Same old thing all the time.

MAN:

My white folks didn't mind their niggers praying and singing hymns, but some places wouldn't 'low them to worship a-tall, and they had to put their heads in pots to sing or pray.

WOMAN:

Once Massa goes to Baton Rouge and brung back a yaller gal dressed in fine style. She was a seamster nigger. He builds her a house 'way from the quarters. This yaller gal breeds fast and gits a mess of white young-uns. She larnt them fine manners and combs out they hair.

Oncet two of them goes down the hill to the dollhouse, where the Missy's children am playing. They wants to go in the dollhouse and one of the Missy's boys say, "That's for white children." They say, "We ain't no niggers, 'cause we got the same daddy as you has, and he comes to see us near every day." They is fussing, and Missy is listening out her chamber window . . .

When Massa come home his wife hardly say nothing to him, and he asks her what the matter, and she tells him, "Since you asks me, I'm studying in my mind 'bout them white young-uns of that yaller nigger wench from Baton Rouge." He say, "Now, honey, I fotches that gal just for you, 'cause she a fine seamster." She say, "It look kind of funny they got the same kind of hair and eyes as my children, and they got a nose look like yours." He say, "Honey, you just paying 'tention to talk of little children that ain't got no mind to what they say." She say, "Over in Mississippi I got a home and plenty with my daddy, and I got that in my mind."

Well, she didn't never leave, and Massa bought her a fine, new span of surrey hosses. But she don't never have no more children, and she ain't so cordial with the Massa. That yaller gal has more white young-uns, but they don't never go down the hill no more.

MAN:

One thing what make it tough on the niggers was them times when a man and he wife and their children had to be taken 'way from one another, sold off or taken 'way to some other state. They was heaps of nigger families that I know what was separated in the time of bondage that tried to find they folkses what was gone. But the mostest of 'em never git together again even after they sot free 'cause they don't know where one or the other is.

MAN:

Slavery time was tough, boss. You just don't know how tough it was. I can't 'splain to you just how bad all the niggers want to get they freedom.

NEGRO ACTRESS (sings):
Right foot, left foot,
Along the road,
Follow the drinking gourd.

Up to the North,
Drop your load,
Follow the drinking gourd.

NARRATOR:
Slaves constantly tried to flee the plantation and head

North to freedom. Efforts by their masters to trace them led, in a few rare cases, to an exchange of letters.

JOURDAN ANDERSON:

To My Old Master, Colonel P. H. Anderson, Big Spring, Tennessee.

Sir: I got your letter, and was glad to find that you had not forgotten Jourdan, and that you wanted me to come back and live with you again. Although you shot at me twice before I left you, I am glad you are still living.

I want to know particularly what the good chance is you propose to give me. I am doing tolerably well here. I get twenty-five dollars a month, with victuals and clothing; have a comfortable home for Mandy,—the folks call her Mrs. Anderson,—and the children—Milly, Jane and Grundy—go to school and are learning well. The teacher says Grundy has a head for a preacher. They go to Sunday school, and Mandy and me attend church regularly. We are kindly treated.

Mandy says she would be afraid to go back without some proof that you were disposed to treat us justly and kindly; and we have concluded to test your sincerity by asking you to send us our wages for the time we served you. This will make us forget and forgive old scores, and rely on your justice and friendship in the future. I served you faithfully for thirty-two years, and Mandy for twenty years. At twenty-five dollars a month for me, and two dollars a week for Mandy, our earnings would amount to eleven thousand six hundred and eighty dollars. Add to this the interest for the time our wages have been kept back, and deduct what you paid for our clothing, and three doctor's visits to me, and pulling a tooth for Mandy, and the balance will show what we are in justice entitled to. Please send the money by Adam's Express, in care of V. Winters, Esq., Dayton, Ohio.

Say howdy to George Carter, and thank him for taking the pistol from you when you were shooting at me.

From your old servant,
Jourdan Anderson

MRS. SARAH LOGUE:

To Jarm: . . . I write you these lines to let you know the situation we are in,—partly in consequence of your running away and stealing Old Rock, our fine mare. Though we got the mare back, she never was worth much after you took her. If you will send me one thousand dollars, and pay for the old mare, I will give up all claim I have to you. In consequence of your running away, we had to sell Abe and Ann and twelve acres of land; and I want you to send me the money, that I may be able to redeem the land. If you do not comply with my request, I will sell you to someone else, and you may rest assured that the time is not far distant when things will be changed with you. A word to the wise is sufficient . . . You know that we reared you as we reared our own children.

Yours, etc
Mrs. Sarah Logue

JARM:

Mrs. Sarah Logue: . . . had you a woman's heart, you never could have sold my only remaining brother and sister, because I put myself beyond your power to convert me into money.

You sold my brother and sister, Abe and Ann, and twelve acres of land . . . Now you ask me to send you $1000 to enable you to redeem the *land,* but not to redeem my poor brother and sister! You say that you shall sell me if I do not send you $1000, and in the same breath you say, "You know we raised you as we did our own children." Woman, did you raise your *own children* for the market? Did you raise them for the whipping post? Did you raise them to be driven off, bound to a coffle in chains? Where are my poor bleeding brothers and sisters? Can you tell? Who was it that sent them off into sugar and cotton fields, to be kicked and cuffed, and whipped, and to groan and die . . . ?

Did you think to terrify me by presenting the alternative to give my money to you, or give my body to slavery? Then let me say to you, that I meet the proposition with scorn and contempt. I will not budge one hair's breadth. I will not breathe a shorter breath . . . I stand among free people.

NARRATOR:
Some Negroes reacted to slavery not by fleeing, but by rising in rebellion. In 1831, the slave Nat Turner, and his followers, turned on their masters in Southampton County, Virginia.

NAT TURNER:
I was thirty-five years of age the second of October last, and born the property of Benjamin Turner. In my childhood a circumstance occurred which made an indelible impression on my mind . . . Being at play with other children, when three or four years old, I was telling them something, which my mother, overhearing, said had happened before I was born. I stuck to my story, however, and related some other things which went, in her opinion, to confirm it. Others being called on, were greatly astonished, and caused them to say, in my hearing, I surely would be a prophet . . .

I studiously avoided mixing in society, and wrapped myself in mystery, devoting my time to fasting and prayer. I obtained influence over the minds of my fellow-servants —(not by the means of conjuring and such-like tricks— for to them I always spoke of such things with contempt), but by the communion of the Spirit . . . they believed and said my wisdom came from God.

About this time I had a vision—I saw white spirits and

black spirits engaged in battle, and the sun was darkened —the thunder rolled in the heavens, and blood flowed in streams—and I heard a voice saying, "Such is your luck, such you are called to see; and let it come rough or smooth, you must surely hear it." I communicated the great work laid out for me to do. It was quickly agreed, neither age nor sex was to be spared.

It was my object to carry terror and devastation wherever we went. We killed Mrs. Waller and ten children. Then we started for Mr. William Williams . . . Mrs. Williams fled, but she was pursued, overtaken, and after showing her the mangled body of her lifeless husband, she was told to get down and lay by his side, where she was shot dead. The white men pursued and fired on us several times. Five or six of my men were wounded, but none left on the field. . . . Finding myself defeated . . . I gave up all hope for the present . . . I was taken, a fortnight afterwards in a little hole I had dug out with my sword. I am here loaded with chains, and willing to suffer the fate that awaits me.

NEGRO ACTOR (*sings*):
For the old man is a waitin!
For to carry you to freedom
If you follow the drinking gourd.

NARRATOR:
In the North, although the Negroes were free, they were segregated and despised. The Reverend Samuel J. May described their treatment in Canterbury, Connecticut.

MAY:
In the summer or fall of 1832 I heard that Miss Prudence Crandall, an excellent, well-educated Quaker, had been induced by a number of ladies and gentlemen of Canterbury, Connecticut to establish her boarding and day school there.

For a while the school answered the expectations of its

patrons, but early in the following year, trouble arose. Not far from Canterbury there lived a colored man named Harris. He had a daughter, Sarah, a bright girl about seventeen years of age. She had passed, with good repute as a scholar, through the school of the district and was hungering for more education. Sarah applied for admission into this new Canterbury school and Miss Crandall admitted her.

The pupils, I believe, made no objection. But in a few days the parents of some of them called and remonstrated. "They would not have it said that their daughters went to school with a nigger girl." Miss Crandall was assured that, if she did not dismiss Sarah Harris, her white pupils would be withdrawn from her.

She could not comply with such a demand . . . Accordingly, she gave notice that next term her school would be opened for "young ladies and little misses of color." The whole town was in a flame of indignation. Miss Crandall begged me to come to her as soon as my engagements would permit. When I arrived I was informed that a town-meeting was to be held. She requested that I might be heard as her attorney.

The Hon. Andrew T. Judson was undoubtedly the chief of Miss Crandall's persecutors. He was the great man of the town, much talked of by the Democrats as soon to be Governor, and a few years afterwards was appointed Judge of the United States District Court.

JUDSON:

Mr. May, we are not merely opposed to the establishment of this school in Canterbury; we mean there shall not be such a school set up anywhere in our State. The colored people never can rise from their menial condition in our country; they ought not to be permitted to rise here. They are an inferior race of beings, and never can or ought to be recognized as the equals of the whites. Africa is the place for them.

MAY:

Mr. Judson, there never will be fewer colored people in this country than there are now. Of the vast majority of them this is the native land, as much as it is ours. The only question is, whether we will recognize the rights which God gave them as men.

JUDSON:

That nigger school shall never be allowed in Canterbury, nor in any town of this State.

MAY (*to audience*):

Undismayed by such opposition, Miss Crandall received early in April fifteen or twenty colored young ladies from Philadelphia, New York, Providence, and Boston. At once all accommodations at the stores in Canterbury were denied her. She and her pupils were insulted whenever they appeared in the streets. The doors and door-steps of her house were besmeared; her well was filled with filth. Finally the house was assaulted by a number of persons with heavy clubs and iron bars; five window-sashes were demolished and ninety panes of glass dashed to pieces.

For the first time Miss Crandall seemed to quail, and her pupils had become afraid to remain another night under her roof. The front rooms of the house were hardly tenantable; and it seemed foolish to repair them only to be destroyed again. After due consideration, therefore, it was determined that the school should be abandoned. The pupils were called together, and I was requested to announce to them our decision. Twenty harmless, well-behaved girls, whose only offence was that they had come together there to obtain useful knowledge, were to be told that they had better go away. The words almost blistered my lips. I felt ashamed of Canterbury, ashamed of Connecticut, ashamed of my country, ashamed of my color.

NARRATOR:

Many Northern Negroes were active in the antislavery struggle, and some took part in other reform movements as well. One of the most famous was the illiterate ex-slave Sojourner Truth, who in 1851 unexpectedly rose at a Woman's Rights Convention.

SOJOURNER TRUTH:

Wall, chilern, whar dar is so much racket dar must be somethin' out o' kilter. I tink dat 'twixt de black folks of de Souf and de womin at de Norf, all talkin' 'bout rights, de white men will be in a fix pretty soon. But what's all dis here talkin' 'bout?

Dat man ober dar say day womin needs to be helped into carriages, and lifted ober ditches, and to hab de best place everywhar. Nobody eber helps me into carriages, or ober mud-puddles, or gibs me any best place! And a'n't I a woman? Look at me! Look at my arm! I have ploughed, and planted, and gathered into barns and no man could head me! And a'n't I a woman? I have borne thirteen chilern, and seen 'em mos' sold off to slavery, and when I cried out with my mother's grief, none but Jesus heard me! And a'n't I a woman?

Den dey talks 'bout dis ting in de head; what dis dey call it? (*A voice whispering*): Intellect.

Dat's it, honey. What's dat got to do wid womin's rights? If my cup won't hold but a pint, and yourn holds a quart, wouldn't ye be mean not to let me have my little half-measure full?

Den dat little man in black dar, he say women can't have as much rights as men, 'cause Christ wan't a woman! Whar did your Christ come from? Whar did your Christ come from? From God and a woman! Man had nothin' to do wid Him!

If de fust woman God ever made was strong enough to

turn de world upside down all alone, dese women to-
gedder ought to be able to turn it back, and get it right
side up again! And now dey is asking to do it, de men
better let 'em.

CAST (*sings*):
God's gonna set this world on fire,
God's gonna set this world on fire
One of these days, halleluja!
God's gonna set this world on fire,
Gonna set this world on fire one of these days.

NARRATOR:
In 1859, John Brown, who has alternately been called a
saint and a madman, made an unsuccessful attempt at
Harpers Ferry, Virginia, to free the slaves. Brought to trial
and sentenced to death, John Brown addressed the court.

JOHN BROWN:
I have, may it please the Court, a few words to say.

In the first place, I deny everything but what I have all
along admitted,—the design on my part to free the slaves.
I never did intend murder, or treason. Had I interfered in
behalf of the rich, the powerful, the intelligent, the so-
called great, it would have been all right; and every man
in this court would have deemed it an act worthy of reward rather than punishment.

This court acknowledges, as I suppose, the validity of the
law of God. I see a book kissed here which I suppose to
be the Bible. That teaches me that all things whatsoever
I would that men should do to me, I should do even so to
them. It teaches me, further, to "remember them that
are in bonds, as bound with them." I endeavored to act
up to that instruction. I say, I am yet too young to understand that God is any respecter of persons. I believe
that to have interfered as I have done—as I have always
freely admitted I have done—in behalf of His despised
poor, was not wrong, but right. Now, if it is deemed

necessary that I should forfeit my life for the furtherance of the ends of justice, and mingle my blood further
with the blood of millions in this slave country—I submit; so let it be done!

NARRATOR:

*Just before John Brown was led from his cell to the gal-
lows, he handed a guard this last message.*

JOHN BROWN:

"I, John Brown, am now quite *certain* that the crimes of
this *guilty land* will never be purged away but with
blood. I had, as I now think vainly, flattered myself that
without very much bloodshed it might be done."
            (*Guitar chords of "John Brown's Body"*)

NARRATOR:

*Civil war broke out in April 1861. Mary Boykin Ches-
nut, wife of the Senator from South Carolina, described
in her diary the onset of war. April 8, 1861 . . .*

MRS. CHESNUT:

Talbot and Chew have come to say that hostilities are to
begin. The men went off almost immediately, and I crept
silently to my room where I sat down to a good cry . . .
Mrs. Wigfall came in and we had it out, on the subject of
civil war. We solaced ourselves with dwelling on all its
known horrors, and then we added some remarks about
what we had a right to expect with Yankees in front
and Negroes in the rear. "The slave owners must expect
a servile insurrection, of course," said Mrs. Wigfall.

NARRATOR:

April 13, 1861 . . .

MRS. CHESNUT:

Fort Sumter has been on fire . . . Not by one word or
look can we detect any change in the demeanor of these
Negro servants. Lawrence sits at our door, as sleepy and
as respectful and as profoundly indifferent. So are they

all. They carry it too far. You could not tell they even hear the awful noise that is going on in the bay, though it is dinning in their ears night and day. And people talk before them as if they were chairs and tables, and they make no sign. Are they stolidly stupid, or wiser than we are, silent and strong, biding their time.

NARRATOR:
August 1863, Portland, Alabama . . .

MRS. CHESNUT:
Dick, the butler here, reminds me that when we were children, I taught him to read as soon as I could read myself . . . but he won't look at me now. He looks over my head, he scents freedom in the air. He always was very ambitious.

He is the first Negro that I have felt a change in. They go about in their black masks, not a ripple or an emotion showing; and yet on all other subjects except the War they are the most excitable of all races. Now Dick might make a very respectable Egyptian Sphinx, so inscrutably silent is he.

(*Guitar effect of drum rolls*)

NARRATOR:
The first regiment of ex-slaves was mustered into the service of the Union Army in 1862. It was under the command of a white officer from Boston, Colonel Thomas Wentworth Higginson.

HIGGINSON:
November 24, 1862 . . . Reporting to General Saxton, I had the luck to encounter a company of my destined command, marched in to be mustered into the United States service. The first to whom I spoke had been wounded in a small expedition after lumber, in which he had been under fire.

(NEGRO SOLDIER *steps forward and stands at attention.*)

(*To* NEGRO SOLDIER): Did you think that more than you bargained for, my man?

NEGRO SOLDIER:

I been a-tinking. Mas'r, *dat's jess what I went for.*

HIGGINSON (*to audience*):

I thought this did well enough for my very first interchange of dialogue with my recruits.

(*Consulting his diary*)

December 5, 1862. This evening, after working themselves up to the highest pitch, a party suddenly rushed off, got a barrel, and mounted some man upon it, who brought out one of the few really impressive appeals for the American flag that I have ever heard . . .

(*The lights dim on* HIGGINSON *and come up on another* NEGRO SOLDIER.)

NEGRO SOLDIER:

Our mas'rs dey hab lib under de flag, dey got dere wealth under it, and ebryting beautiful for dere chilen. Under it dey hab grind us up, and put us in dere pocket for money. But de fus' minute dey tink dat ole flag mean freedom for we colored people, dey pull it right down, and run up de rag ob dere own. But we'll nebber desert de ole flag, boys, neber; we hab lib under it for *eighteen hundred sixty-two years,* and we'll die for it now.

(*Lights fade on the* SOLDIER *and come up on* HIGGINSON.)

HIGGINSON:

Their religious spirit grows more beautiful to me in living longer with them. Imbued from childhood with the habit of submission, they can endure everything. Their religion also gives them zeal, energy, daring. They could easily be made fanatics, if I chose; but I do not choose. Their whole mood is essentially Mohammedan, perhaps, in its strength and its weakness. The white camps seem rough and secular, after this; and I hear our men talk about "a religious army," "a Gospel army," in their prayer-meetings. They are certainly evangelizing the chaplain, who was rather a heretic at the beginning . . .

1ST NEGRO SOLDIER (*praying*):

Let me lib dat when I die I shall *hab manners,* dat I shall know what to say when I see my Heabenly Lord.

2nd NEGRO SOLDIER (*praying*):

Let me lib wid de musket in one hand an' de Bible in de oder,—dat if I die at de muzzle ob de musket, I may know I hab de bressed Jesus in my hand, an' hab no fear.

3rd NEGRO SOLDIER (*praying*):

I hab lef' my wife in de land o' bondage; my little ones dey say eb'ry night, Whar is my fader? But when I die, when I shall stan' in de glory, den, O Lord, I shall see my wife an' my little chil'en once more.

HIGGINSON:

Expedition up the St. Mary's River: This morning, my surgeon sent me his report of killed and wounded: "One man killed instantly by a ball through the heart, and seven wounded, one of whom will die. Robert Sutton, with three wounds,—one of which, being on the skull, may cost him his life—would not report himself till compelled to do so by his officers."

    (*He puts away the surgeon's report.*)

And one of those who were carried to the vessel—a man wounded through the lungs—asked only if I were safe, the contrary having been reported. An officer may be pardoned some enthusiasm for such men as these . . .

    (*He turns to another page in the diary.*)

January 1, 1863. Today we celebrated the issuance of President Lincoln's Proclamation of Emancipation. It was read by Dr. W. H. Brisbane. Then the colors were presented to us by the Rev. Mr. French. All this was according to the programme. Then, the very moment the speaker had ceased, and just as I took and waved the flag . . .

NEGRO SINGERS (*breaking in*):
My Country, 'tis of thee,
Sweet land of liberty,
Of thee I sing!

(*The singing continues quietly under the rest of the speech.*)

HIGGINSON:
Firmly the quavering voices sang on, verse after verse; others of the colored people joined in; some whites on the platform began, but I motioned them to silence. I never saw anything so electric; it made all other words cheap; it seemed the choked voice of a race at last unloosed. Just think of it!—the first day they had ever had a country, the first flag they had ever seen which promised anything to their people! When they stopped, there was nothing to do for it but to speak, and I went on; but the life of the whole day was in those unknown people's song.

(*The singing swells.*)

SINGERS:
. . . From every mountainside
Let freedom ring!

Act 2

ACT 2

NEGRO ACTOR:

No more auction block for me,
No more, no more,
No more auction block for me,
Many thousand gone.

No more pint of salt for me,
No more, no more,
No more pint of salt for me,
Many thousand gone.

NEGRO MAN:

We was free. Just like that, we was free. Right off colored folks started on the move. They seemed to want to get closer to freedom, so they'd know what it was—like it was a place or a city . . .

NEGRO WOMAN:

A heap of people say they going to name theirselves over. They name theirselves big names. Some of the names was Abraham, and some called theirselves Lincum. Any big name 'cepting their master's name.

NEGRO MAN:

The slaves don't know where to go. They's always 'pend on Old Marse to look after them. Three families went to get farms for theyselves, but the rest stay on for hands on the old place.

NEGRO WOMAN:

I remember someone asking—"You got to say 'Master'?" And somebody answered and said, "Naw." But they said it all the same. They said it for a long time.

NEGRO MAN:

They makes us git right off the place, just like you take a old hoss and turn it loose. That how us was. No money, no nothing.

NEGRO MAN:

What I likes best, to be slave or free? Well, it's this way. In slavery I owns nothing and never owns nothing. In freedom I's own the home and raise the family. All that cause me worriment, and in slavery I has no worriment, but I takes the freedom.

NARRATOR:

The whites reacted to the Negroes' freedom in a variety of ways. A Northern woman, Elizabeth Bothume, went South to teach the ex-slaves.

ELIZABETH BOTHUME:

On Oct. 25, 1864, I received the following communication:—"You are hereby appointed by the New England Freedman's Aid Society a teacher of freed people at Beaufort, South Carolina." I found my location was to be at Old Fort Plantation. A large number of colored refugees had been brought here and I was impatient to begin. Each hour showed me that at the North we had but a faint conception of the work to be done.

While the zeal of these people for learning never flags, they have no possible conception of time. Men, women and children hurry to the schoolhouse at all hours and at most unseasonable times, expecting "to catch a lesson." Reproof is unheeded, or not understood; "Us had something *particular* to do," is the invariable excuse.

I must confess, the ignorance of some of the visitors in regard to the condition of the freedman is positively astounding. Some officers belonging to the "Tenth Army Corps" of Sherman's army visited the school. I was expecting them, and had examined the children a little upon general subjects. Imagine my surprise, when they had sung and answered a few general questions, to have one of the visitors get up and ask, "Children, who is Jesus Christ?" For a moment the whole school seemed paralyzed. Then an older boy sprang up, and exclaimed, "Him's Massa Linkum" . . .

Then General Howard made a short address, in which he gave them a motto, "To try hard." This all could understand. So when he asked what he should tell their friends at the North about them, they all answered, "Tell 'em we'se goin' to try hard."

At another school General Howard asked this question, and a little boy answered, "Massa, tell 'em we is rising."

NARRATOR:
The Negroes' freedom disrupted the pattern of Southern life, as a Georgia woman, Eliza Andrews, noted in her diary.

ELIZA ANDREWS:
Washington, Georgia. No power on earth can raise an inferior, savage race above their civilized masters and keep them there. No matter how high a prop they build under him, the negro is obliged, sooner or later, to find his level. The higher above his natural capacity they force the negro in their rash experiments, the greater must be his fall in the end, and the more bitter our sufferings in the meantime.

The town is becoming more crowded with "freedmen" every day, and their insolence increases with their numbers. We have not even an errand boy now, for George, the only child left on the place, is going to school! . . . Everybody is doing housework. Father says this is what has made the Anglo-Saxon race great; they are not afraid of work. But it does seem to me a waste of time for people who are capable of doing something better to spend their time sweeping and dusting while scores of lazy negroes that are fit for nothing else are lying around idle. Dr. Calhoun suggested that it would be a good idea to import some of those apes from Africa and teach them to take the place of the negroes, but Henry said that just as soon as we had got them tamed, and taught them to be of some use, those crazy fanatics at the North would insist on coming down here to emancipate them and give them universal suffrage. A good many people seem to think that the Yankees are never going to be satisfied till they get the negroes to voting. Father says it is the worst thing we have to fear now.

(*Guitar chords of "Dixie"*)

NARRATOR:

By 1866, the voting question was paramount. On February 7, Frederick Douglass, the chief spokesman for his race, and George T. Downing, another prominent Negro leader, brought the issue to Andrew Johnson, President of the United States.

GEORGE T. DOWNING:

We present ourselves to your Excellency in the name of the colored people of the United States. We are Americans, native born Americans. We are citizens. On this fact, and with confidence in the triumph of justice, we cherish the hope that we may be fully enfranchised.

PRESIDENT JOHNSON:

I do not like to be arraigned by some who can get up handsomely-rounded periods and deal in rhetoric. While I say I am a friend of the colored man, I do not want to adopt a policy that I believe will end in a contest between the races, in the extermination of one or the other. God forbid that I should be engaged in such a work!

FREDERICK DOUGLASS:
Mr. President, do you wish—

PRESIDENT JOHNSON:
I am not quite through yet . . . The query comes up, whether these two races without time for passion and excitement to be appeased, and without time for the slightest improvement, are to be thrown together at the ballot-box.

Will you say a majority of the people shall receive a state of things they are opposed to?

DOUGLASS:
That was said before the war.

JOHNSON:
I am now talking about a principle; not what somebody else said.

DOWNING:
Apply what you have said, Mr. President, to South Carolina, where a majority of the inhabitants are colored.

JOHNSON:
That doesn't change the principle at all. It is for the people to say who shall vote, and not for the Congress of the United States. It is a fundamental tenet in my creed that the will of the people must be obeyed. Is there anything wrong or unfair in that?

DOUGLASS (SMILING):
A great deal that is wrong, Mr. President, with all respect.

JOHNSON:

It is the people of the States that must for themselves determine this thing.

God knows that anything I can do to elevate the races I will do, and to be able to do so is the sincere desire of my heart. (*abruptly*) I am glad to have met you, and thank you for the compliments you have paid me.

DOUGLASS:

I have to return to you our thanks, Mr. President, for so kindly granting us this interview. We did not come here expecting to argue this question with your excellency . . . if you would grant us permission, of course we would endeavor to controvert some of the positions you have assumed.

JOHNSON:

I thought you expected me to indicate what my views were on the subjects touched upon by your statement.

DOWNING:

We are very happy, indeed, to have heard them.

DOUGLASS:

If the President will allow me, I would like to say one or two words in reply. You enfranchise your enemies and disfranchise your friends.

JOHNSON:

All I have done is to indicate what my views are, as I supposed you expected me to, from your address.

DOUGLASS:

But if your excellency will be pleased to hear, I would like to say a word or two in regard to enfranchisement of the blacks as a means of *preventing* a conflict of races.

JOHNSON:

I repeat, I merely wanted to indicate my views, and not to enter into any general controversy.

Your statement was a very frank one, and I thought it was due to you to meet it in the same spirit.

DOUGLASS:

Thank you, sir.

JOHNSON:

If you will all inculcate the idea that the colored people can live and advance to better advantage elsewhere than in the South, it would be better for them.

DOUGLASS:

But we cannot get away from the plantation.

JOHNSON:

What prevents you?

DOUGLASS:

The Negro is divested of all power. He is absolutely in the hands of those men.

JOHNSON:

If the master now controls him or his action, would he not control him in his vote?

DOUGLASS:

Let the Negro once understand that he has an organic right to vote, and he will raise up a party in the Southern States among the poor, who will rally with him.

JOHNSON:

I suggest emigration. If he cannot get employment in the South, he has it in his power to go where he can get it.

DOUGLASS (*to his fellow delegates*):

The President sends us to the people and we go to the people.

JOHNSON:

Yes, sir; I have great faith in the people. I believe they will do what is right.

(*Music—guitarist*)
I am a good old Rebel,
And that's just what I am.
And for this land of liberty,
I do not give a damn.
I'm glad I fought against it—
I only wish we'd won,
And I ain't askin pardon,
For what I been or done.

(*As the lights fade on the scene, they come up on the figure of a man wearing the hood of the Ku Klux Klan.*)

NARRATOR:

In 1866, the Radical wing of the Republican party gained control of Congress and gave the Negro the right to vote. At once, the Ku Klux Klan rose to power in the South . . .

THE HOODED FIGURE:

Before the immaculate Judge of Heaven and Earth, and upon the Holy Evangelists of Almighty God, I do, of my own free will and accord, subscribe to the sacredly binding obligation: We are on the side of justice, humanity and constitutional liberty, as bequeathed to us in its purity by our forefathers. We oppose and reject the principles of the Radical party.

(*Music—guitarist*)
I hate the Freedmen's Bureau
And the uniform of blue,
I hate the Declaration of Independence, too.
I hate the Constitution
With all its fume and fuss,
And them thievin', lyin' Yankees,
Well, I hate 'em wuss and wuss.

NARRATOR:

Acts of violence by the Klan were investigated by the Federal government in a series of hearings and trials.

PROSECUTOR:

What was the purpose of the Ku Klux Klan? What were the raids for?

KLANSMAN:

To put down Radicalism, the raids were for.

PROSECUTOR:

In what way were they to put down Radicalism?

KLANSMAN:

It was to whip them and make them change their politics.

PROSECUTOR:

How many raids have you been on by order of the Chief?

KLANSMAN:

Two, sir.

PROSECUTOR:

Now, will you state to the jury what was done on those raids?

KLANSMAN:

Yes, sir. We were ordered to meet at Howl's Ferry, and went and whipped five colored men. Presley Holmes was the first they whipped, and then went on and whipped Jerry Thompson; went then and whipped Charley Good, James Leach, and Amos Lowell.

PROSECUTOR:

How many men were on these raids?

KLANSMAN:

I think there was twenty in number.

PROSECUTOR:

How were they armed and uniformed?

KLANSMAN:

They had red gowns, and had white covers over thei
horses. Some had pistols and some had guns.

PROSECUTOR:

What did they wear on their heads?

KLANSMAN:

Something over their heads came down. Some of them
had horns on.

PROSECUTOR:

Disguises dropped down over their faces?

KLANSMAN:

Yes, sir.

PROSECUTOR:

What was the object in whipping those five men you have
named?

KLANSMAN:

The object, in whipping Presley Holmes, was about some
threats he had made about him going to be buried in
Salem graveyard.

PROSECUTOR:

What was the first to occur?

KLANSMAN:

Well, sir, Webber—he was leading the Klan—ran into
the yard and kicked down the door, and dragged him
out, and led him off about two hundred yards, and
whipped him.

PROSECUTOR:

How many lashes did they give him?

KLANSMAN:

I cannot tell you how many.

PROSECUTOR:

Did they whip him severely or not?

KLANSMAN:

His shirt was stuck to his back.

PROSECUTOR:

What occurred at the next place?

KLANSMAN:

They whipped Jerry Thompson at the next place; told him never to go to any more meetings; to stay at home and attend to his own business.

PROSECUTOR:

What was done at the next place?

KLANSMAN:

They went there and whipped Charley Good. They whipped him very severe; they beat him with a pole and kicked him down on the ground.

PROSECUTOR:

What did they tell him?

KLANSMAN:

To let Radicalism alone; if he didn't his doom would be fatal.

(*The lights fade. They come up immediately on another examination. A Negro woman,* HANNAH TUTSON, *is being questioned.*)

LAWYER:

Are you the wife of Samuel Tutson?

MRS. TUTSON:

Yes, sir.

LAWYER:

Were you at home when he was whipped last spring?

MRS. TUTSON:

Yes, sir; I was at home.

LAWYER:

Tell us what took place then, what was done, and how it was done.

MRS. TUTSON:

That night, just as I got into bed, five men bulged right against the door, and it fell in the middle of the floor. George McRae ran right to me. As I saw him coming I took up the child—the baby—and held to him. I started to scream, and George McRae catched me by the throat and choked me. And he catched the little child by the foot and slinged it out of my arms. They got me out of doors. The old man was ahead of me, and I saw Dave Donley stamp on him. They carried me to a pine, and then they tied my hands there. They pulled off all my linen, tore it up so that I did not have a piece of rag on me as big as my hand. I said, "Men what are you going to do with me?" They said, "God damn you, we will show you; you are living on another man's premises." I said, "No; I am living on my own premises; I gave $150 for it and Captain Buddington and Mr. Mundy told me to stay here." They whipped me for awhile. Then George McRae would say, "Come here, True-Klux." Then the True-Klux would step off about as far as (*pointing to a member of the committee*) that gentleman and whisper; when they came back they would whip me again. Every time they would go off, George McRae would make me squat down by the pine, and he would get his knees between my legs and say, "Old lady, if you don't let me have to do with you, I will kill you." I said, "No"; they whipped me. There were four men whipping me at once.

LAWYER:

How many lashes did they give you in all?

MRS. TUTSON:

I cannot tell you, for they whipped me from the crown of my head to the soles of my feet. I was just raw. After I got away from them that night I ran to my house. My house was torn down. I went in and felt where my bed was. I could not feel my little children and I could not see them.

LAWYER:

Did you find your children?

MRS. TUTSON:

I did next day at 12 o'clock.

LAWYER:

Where were they?

MRS. TUTSON:

They went out into the field.

LAWYER:

Did the baby get hurt—the one you had in your arms when they jerked it away?

MRS. TUTSON:

Yes, sir; in one of its hips. When it began to walk one of its hips was very bad, and every time you would stand it up it would scream. But I rubbed it and rubbed it, and it looks like he is outgrowing it now.

(Music—Guitarist)
You've got to cross that lonesome valley,
You've got to cross it by yourself.
There ain't nobody can do it for you,
You've got to cross it all alone.

NARRATOR:

The Federal investigations were not followed by effective Federal action. From 1878 to 1915 over 3000 Negroes were lynched in the South—a necessary protection, it was said, against Negro rapists. Yet most lynchings were either for no offense or for such causes as "Insult," "Bad Reputation," "Running Quarantine," "Frightening Children by Shooting at Rabbits," or "Mistaken Identity."

On January 21, 1907, United States Senator Ben Tillman, of South Carolina, gave his views on the subject from the Senate floor.

SENATOR TILLMAN:

Mr. President, a word about lynching and my attitude toward it. A great deal has been said in the newspapers, North and South, about my responsibility in connection with this matter.

I have justified it for one crime, and one only. As governor of South Carolina I proclaimed that, although I had taken the oath of office to support law and enforce it, I would lead a mob to lynch any man who had ravished a woman.

Mr. President . . . When stern and sad-faced white men put to death a creature in human form who has deflowered a white woman, they have avenged the greatest wrong, the blackest crime in all the category of crimes.

The Senator from Wisconsin prates about the law. Look at our environment in the South, surrounded and in a very large number of counties outnumbered, by the negroes—engulfed, as it were, in a black flood of semi-barbarians. For forty years these negroes have been taught the damnable heresy of equality with the white man. Their minds are those of children, while they have the passions and strength of men.

Let us carry the Senator from Wisconsin to the back-woods in South Carolina, put him on a farm miles from a town or railroad, and environed with negroes. We will suppose he has a fair young daughter just budding into womanhood; and recollect this, the white women of the South are in a state of siege . . .

That Senator's daughter undertakes to visit a neighbor or is left home alone for a brief while. Some lurking demon who has watched for the opportunity seizes her; she is choked or beaten into insensibility and ravished, her body prostituted, her purity destroyed, her chastity taken from her, and a memory branded on her brain as with a red-hot iron to haunt her night and day as long as she lives.

In other words, a death in life. This young girl thus blighted and brutalized drags herself to her father and tells him what has happened. Is there a man here with red blood in his veins who doubts what impulses the father would feel? Is it any wonder that the whole countryside rises as one man and with set, stern faces, seek the brute who has wrought this infamy? And shall such a creature, because he has the semblance of a man, appeal to the law? Shall men coldbloodedly stand up and demand for him the right to have a fair trial and be punished in the regular course of justice? So far as I am concerned he has put himself outside the pale of the law, human and divine. He has sinned against the Holy Ghost. He has invaded the holy of holies. He has struck civilization a blow, the most deadly and cruel that the imagination can conceive. It is idle to reason about it; it is idle to preach about it. Our brains reel under the staggering blow and hot blood surges to the heart. Civilization peels off us, any and all of us who are men, and we revert to the original savage type whose impulses under such circumstances has always been to "kill! kill! kill!"

NARRATOR:

The Negro's intimidation was reflected in the views of Mr. Booker T. Washington, the most prominent Negro at the turn of the century, when he addressed a predominantly white audience in Atlanta.

WASHINGTON:

The Negroes' greatest danger is, that in the great leap from slavery to freedom we may overlook the fact that the masses of us are to live by the production of our hands. It is at the bottom of life we must begin, and not the top. You can be sure in the future, as you have been in the past, that you and your families will be surrounded by the most patient, faithful, law-abiding, and unresentful people that the world has seen.

In all things that are purely social we can be as separate as the fingers, yet one as the hand in all things essential to mutual progress.

The wisest among my race understand that the agitation of questions of social equality is the extremist folly. It is important and right that all privileges of the law be ours, but it is vastly more important that we be prepared for the exercise of those privileges. The opportunity to earn a dollar in a factory just now is worth infinitely more than the opportunity to spend a dollar in an opera house.

NARRATOR:

W. E. B. DuBois, later one of the founders of the N.A.A.C.P., was not satisfied with Mr. Washington's leadership.

DUBOIS:

One hesitates to criticise a life which, beginning with so little, has done so much. And yet the time is come when one may speak in all sincerity and utter courtesy of the mistakes and short-comings of Mr. Booker T. Washington. Mr. Washington represents in Negro thought the old attitude of adjustment and submission. He practically accepts the alleged inferiority of the Negro races and withdraws many of the high demands of Negroes as men and American citizens. Mr. Washington asks that black people concentrate all their energies on industrial education, the accumulation of wealth and the conciliation of the South.

We do not expect that the free right to vote, to enjoy civic rights, and to be educated, will come in a moment; we do not expect to see the bias and prejudices of years disappear at the blast of a trumpet; but we are absolutely certain that the way for a people to gain their reasonable rights is not by voluntarily throwing them away and insisting that they do not want them; that the way for a people to gain respect is not by continually belittling and ridiculing themselves; that, on the contrary, Negroes must insist, in season and out of season, that voting is necessary to modern manhood, that color discrimination is barbarism, and that black boys need education as well as white boys.

NARRATOR:

The segregation of Federal employees became widespread for the first time during Woodrow Wilson's administration. To protest this policy, a delegation of Negro leaders, led by Monroe Trotter, called upon President Wilson in November 1914.

MONROE TROTTER:

Mr. President, one year ago we came before you and presented a national petition, signed by colored Americans in thirty-eight states, protesting against the segregation of employees of the National Government as instituted under your administration. We come to you, Mr. President, a year after to renew the protest and appeal.

PRESIDENT WILSON:

After our last visit, I and my cabinet officers investigated as promised, and my cabinet officers told me the segregation was caused by friction between colored and white clerks, and not done to injure or humiliate the colored clerks, but to avoid friction. Members of the cabinet have assured me that the colored clerks would have comfortable conditions, though separated. The white people of the country, as well as I, wish to see the colored people progress, admire the progress they have already made, and want to see them continue along independent lines. There is, however, a great prejudice against colored people, and we must deal with it as practical men. Segregation is not humiliating but a benefit, and ought to be so regarded by you gentlemen. If your organization goes out and tells the colored people of the country that it is a humiliation, they will so regard it.

TROTTER (*angrily*):

Mr. President, it is not in accord with known facts to claim that segregation was started because of race friction of the white and colored clerks, for the simple reason that for fifty years white and colored clerks have been working together in peace and harmony and friendliness, doing so even through two Democratic administrations. Soon after your inauguration began segregation was drastically introduced.

WILSON:

If this organization is ever to have another hearing before me it must have another spokesman. Your manner offends me.

TROTTER:

In what way?

WILSON:

Your tone, with its background of passion.

TROTTER:

But I have no passion in me, Mr. President, you are entirely mistaken; you misinterpret my earnestness for passion. We cannot control the minds of the colored people

and would not if we could on the segregation question.
Two years ago you were regarded as a second Abraham
Lincoln.

WILSON:
I want no personal reference.

TROTTER:
Sir, if you will allow me to continue you will see my intent.

WILSON:
I am the one to do the interrupting, Mr. Trotter.

TROTTER:
We colored leaders are denounced in the colored
churches as traitors to our race.

WILSON:
What do you mean by traitors?

TROTTER:
Because we supported the Democratic ticket in 1912.

WILSON:
Gentlemen, the interview is at an end.

NARRATOR:
*During World War I the French, at the request of the
American authorities, issued a directive concerning Ne-
gro American Troops.*

FRENCH OFFICER:
To the French Military Mission stationed with the
American Army. August 7, 1918. Secret information
concerning the Black American Troops.

It is important for French officers who have been called
upon to exercise command over black American troops,
or to live in close contact with them, to recognize that

American opinion is unanimous on the "color question," and does not admit of any discussion.

The French public has become accustomed to treating the Negro with familiarity and indulgence.

These are matters of grievous concern to the Americans. They consider them an affront to their national policy. It is of the utmost importance that every effort be made to avoid profoundly estranging American opinion.

We must not eat with the blacks, must not shake hands or seek to talk or meet with them outside of the requirements of military service. Americans become greatly incensed at any public expression of intimacy between white women with black men.

Military authority cannot intervene directly in this question, but it can through the civil authorities exercise some influence on the population.

[Signed] Linard

(*Guitar*—"*Mademoiselle from Armentières*")

NARRATOR:
After World War I, Negro resentment became more vocal. Marcus Garvey's movement of Black Nationalism, a forerunner of today's Black Muslims, attracted hundreds of thousands of followers.

MARCUS GARVEY:
We are too large and great in numbers not to be a great people, a great race, and a great nation. We are the descendants of a suffering people. We are the descendants of a people determined to suffer no longer. The time has now come when we must seek our place in the sun. If Europe is for the Europeans, then Africa shall be for the black peoples of the world. We are not asking all the Negroes of the United States to leave for Africa. The majority of us may remain here, but we must send our scientists, our mechanics, and our artizans, and let them

build railroads, let them build the great educational and other institutions necessary, and when they are constructed, the time will come for the command to be given, "Come Home!"

The hour has come for the Negro to take his own initiative. No more fear, no more cringing, no more sycophantic begging and pleading. Destiny leads us to liberty, to freedom; that freedom that Victoria of England never gave; that liberty that Lincoln never meant; that freedom, that liberty, that will see us men among men, that will make us a great and powerful people.

NEGRO ACTRESS (*sings*):
*I'm on my way
To Canaan's land,
I'm on my way
To Canaan's land.*

*I'm on my way
To Canaan's land,
I'm on my way,
Good Lord, I'm on my way.*

NARRATOR:
Out of the difficult years of the Depression emerged the colorful personality of Father Divine. His blend of religion, charity and personal drama brought him thousands of Negro and white followers.

MISS BEAUTIFUL LOVE:
Peace, my dearest Father:
I thank You for allowing me to write as it is my deepest desire to try to please You more each minute. I thank You for Your world at large and Your beautiful, sweet Peace that You have given to all of the children.

I thank you to report some cases of retribution, Father.

There is one whose name is Yaddy, who used dirty words.

He stated You were a little bigger sport than he was. His wife has given birth to a baby who has never closed its mouth. I saw the baby when it was about 9 months old and its mouth hung open very wide.

There is one whose name is Mr. James Barr, who also thinks he is cursing You. He and his truck fell 20 feet below the level . . . He was sent to the hospital . . . now he is going blind.

Father, I will try to please you each day. I will try to make you as happy as the rambling piano keys on Easter Sunday morning, or a happy angel when she does a holy dance.

> Very truly yours,
> Miss Beautiful Love

FATHER DIVINE:

My dear Miss Love:

You can see in every instance that those who tried to measure ME with the measure of a man received the reward meted out to finite man.

In the case of the man, who you say, classed ME with himself, retribution came to him. For it was retribution when his child was born its mouth wide open and cannot close it.

The man, who you say thought he could curse ME suffered retribution and is going blind. Things don't just happen, but they happen Just! What he intended for me came to him heaped up, pressed down and running over.

Thus, retribution rolls on, striking here and there at those who think they can criticize and slander ME, but none can reach ME. Hence, it does not pay to defy MY Name, for this leaves ME, as I AM ever Well, Healthy, Joyful, Peaceful, Lively, Loving, Successful, Prosperous and Happy in Spirit, Body and Mind and in every organ, muscle, sinew, joint, limb, vein and bone and even in every ATOM, fibre and cell of MY BODILY FORM.

Respectfully and Sincere, I AM
REV. M. J. DIVINE, MsD., D.D.
(Better known as FATHER DIVINE)

(*Guitar—reprise of "I'm on My Way"*)

NARRATOR:

As the rest of the nation began to recover from the Depression, Negroes continued to be economically exploited.

LABORER:

I was born in Elbert County, Georgia. I never went to school a day in my life. When I reached twenty-one I signed a contract—that is, I made my mark—to work on a farm for one year. My white employer was to give me $3.50 a week, and furnish me a little house on the plantation. All the people called him Senator. At the end of the first year, the Senator suggested that I sign up a contract for ten years; then, he said, we wouldn't have to fix up papers every year. I asked my wife about it; she consented; and so I made a ten-year contract.

It was then made plain to us that in the contracts, we had agreed to be locked up in a stockade at any time the Senator saw fit. And if we got mad and ran away, we could be run down by bloodhounds, and the Senator might administer any punishment he thought proper. What could we do about it? We shut our mouths, and went to work.

But at the close of the ten-year period, to a man, we all wanted to quit. We refused to sign new contracts—even for one year. But two or three years before, the Senator had started a large store, which was called the commissary. All of us laborers were forced to buy our supplies—food, clothing and so on—from that store. We were charged all sorts of high prices.

Well, at the close of the tenth year, when we meant to

leave, the Senator said to some of us with a smile—and
I never will forget that smile—I can see it now . . .
(*Lights up on two white men, the* SENATOR *and his*
STOREKEEPER. *The* STOREKEEPER *is holding an account
book.*)

SENATOR:

Boys, I'm sorry you're going to leave me. I hope you will
do well in your new places—so well that you will be
able to pay the little balances which most of you owe me.
(*He turns to the* STOREKEEPER, *who steps forward
and reads from the account book.*)

STOREKEEPER:

Frank Raines: One hundred and seventy-three dollars.
Joe Simpson: One hundred and forty-six dollars. Cato
Brown: One hundred and ninety-eight dollars . . .
(*The lights fade on the two white men.*)

LABORER:

According to the books there was no man who owed
less than $100. I owed $165, according to the book-
keeper. No one of us would have dared to dispute a
white man's word. We were told we might go, if we
signed acknowledgments. We would have signed anything, just to get away. So we stepped up and made our
marks. The next morning it was explained to us that in
the papers we had signed we had not only made acknowledgments of our debt, but had also agreed to work
for our employer until the debts were paid by hard labor.
And from that day forward we were treated just like
convicts. Really we had made ourselves slaves, or peons,
as the laws called us.

The working day on a peon farm begins with sunrise
and ends when the sun goes down. Hot or cold, sun or
rain, this is the rule. It was a hard school that peon
camp was. A favorite way of whipping a man was to
strap him down to a log and spank him fifty or sixty

times on his bare feet with a piece of plank. I could tell more, but I've said enough ...

But I didn't tell you how I got out. When I had served for nearly three years—and you remember I owed them only $165—one of the bosses came up to me and said that my time was up. He was the one who was said to be living with my wife. He took me in a buggy into South Carolina, set me down and told me to "git." I been here in the Birmingham district since and I reckon I'll die either in a coal mine or an iron furnace. It don't make much difference which. Either is better than a Georgia peon camp.

(*Guitar—a few bars of "Sometimes I Feel Like a Motherless Child"*)

NARRATOR:
When the Second World War began, segregation was still the official policy of the United States armed forces. It remained so throughout the war. Persistent rumors of conflict between Negro and white troops reached Walter White, Secretary of the N.A.A.C.P., who went overseas to investigate. Among the places he visited was Guam.

WALTER WHITE:
There were no Negro combat troops in Guam, only service units. Negro resentment at this would probably never have been translated into action had not a long series of unchecked and unpunished insults and attacks been made upon these Negroes. Stones, empty beer bottles, and other missiles were thrown from trucks into the Negro camp accompanied by such epithets as "niggers," "night-fighters" and "black sons-of-bitches." Twice hand grenades were hurled into the Negro camp. Small gangs of Marines began to run Negroes out of Agana, the largest town on Guam.

On the afternoon of Christmas Day, 1944, two intoxicated Marines shot and killed a Negro sailor. Neither of them was even arrested . . .

Around nightfall, a jeep with a machine gun mounted on it drove past firing into the Negro camp. By this time the camp was in a state of almost hysterical apprehension. Negroes climbed aboard two trucks and set out for Agana. A road block was thrown up and all of the Negro men—forty-four in number—were arrested . . .

Among the crimes charged against them were unlawful assemblage, rioting, theft of government property, and attempted murder. The recommendations of the Board of Inquiry, despite the evidence, resulted in courts-martial and the sentencing of all forty-four men to prison terms. Happily these were later reversed when we appealed the convictions. But we had to take the cases all the way to the Secretary of the Navy and the White House to achieve this.

It was this pattern which was responsible for the cynical remark I heard so often from Negro troops—"We know that our battle for democracy will begin when we reach San Francisco on our way home!"

NARRATOR:
There was no major breakthrough until 1954, when the Supreme Court declared segregation in public schools unconstitutional. Southern resistance to the court's decision came to a head three years later at Little Rock, Arkansas, when a fifteen-year-old girl tried to go to school at Central High.

GIRL:
The night before I was so excited I couldn't sleep. The next morning I was about the first one up. While I was pressing my black and white dress—I had made it to wear on the first day of school—my little brother turned on the TV set. They started telling about a large crowd gathered at the school. The man on TV said he won-

dered if we were going to show up that morning. Mother called from the kitchen, where she was fixing breakfast, "Turn that TV off!" She was so upset and worried. I wanted to comfort her, so I said, "Mother, don't worry!"

Dad was walking back and forth, from room to room, with a sad expression. He was chewing on his pipe and he had a cigar in his hand, but he didn't light either one. It would have been funny, only he was so nervous.

Before I left home Mother called us into the living room. She said we should have a word of prayer. Then I caught the bus and got off a block from the school. I saw a large crowd of people standing across the street from the soldiers guarding Central. As I walked on, the crowd suddenly got very quiet. For a moment all I could hear was the shuffling of their feet. Then someone shouted, "Here she comes, get ready!" The crowd moved in closer and then began to follow me, calling me names. I still wasn't afraid. Just a little bit nervous. Then my knees started to shake all of a sudden and I wondered whether I could make it to the center entrance a block away. It was the longest block I ever walked in my whole life.

Even so, I still wasn't too scared because all the time I kept thinking that the guards would protect me.

When I got right in front of the school, I went up to a guard. He just looked straight ahead and didn't move to let me pass him. I stood looking at the school—it looked so big! Just then the guards let some white students go through.

The crowd was quiet. I guess they were waiting to see what was going to happen. When I was able to steady my knees, I walked up to the guard who had let the white students in. He too didn't move. When I tried to squeeze past him, he raised his bayonet and then the other guards closed in and they raised their bayonets.

They glared at me with a mean look and I was very frightened and didn't know what to do. I turned around and the crowd came toward me.

They moved closer and closer. Somebody started yelling, "Lynch her!" "Lynch her!"

I tried to see a friendly face somewhere in the mob— someone who maybe would help. I looked into the face of an old woman and it seemed a kind face, but when I looked at her again, she spat on me.

They came closer, shouting, "No nigger bitch is going to get in our school. Get out of here!" Then I looked down the block and saw a bench at the bus stop. I thought, "If I can only get there I will be safe." I don't know why the bench seemed a safe place to me, but I started walking toward it. I tried to close my mind to what they were shouting, and kept saying to myself, "If I can only make it to the bench I will be safe."

When I finally got there, I don't think I could have gone another step. I sat down and the mob crowded up and began shouting all over again. Someone hollered, "Drag her over to this tree! Let's take care of the nigger." Just then a white man sat down beside me, put his arm around me and patted my shoulder.

(During last part of speech, white actor sits beside her on bench.)

WHITE MAN:
She just sat there, her head down. Tears were streaming down her cheeks. I don't know what made me put my arm around her, saying, "Don't let them see you cry." Maybe she reminded me of my 15-year-old daughter.

Just then the city bus came and she got on. She must have been in a state of shock. She never uttered a word.

GIRL:

I can't remember much about the bus ride, but the next thing I remember I was standing in front of the School for the Blind, where Mother works. I ran upstairs and I kept running until I reached Mother's classroom.

Mother was standing at the window with her head bowed, but she must have sensed I was there because she turned around. She looked as if she had been crying, and I wanted to tell her I was all right. But I couldn't speak. She put her arms around me and I cried.

WHITE ACTOR (*sings*):
> *They say down in Hines County*
> *No neutrals can be met,*
> *You'll be a Freedom Rider,*
> *Or a thug for Ross Barnett.*

(WHOLE CAST, *looking at each other, not the audience, quietly sings four lines of "Which Side Are You On"*)

NARRATOR:
After 1957, the Negro protest exploded—bus boycotts, sit-ins, Freedom Rides, drives for voter registration, job protests.

NEGRO MAN:
After 400 years of barbaric treatment, the American Negro is fed up with the unmitigated hypocrisy of the white man.

WHITE MAN:
The Negroes are demanding something that isn't so unreasonable.

NEGRO MAN:
To have a cup of coffee at a lunch counter.

WHITE MAN:
To get a decent job.

NEGRO WOMAN:

The Negro American has been waiting upon voluntary action since 1876.

WHITE MAN:

If the thirteen colonies had waited for voluntary action this land today would be part of the British Commonwealth.

WHITE WOMAN:

The demonstrations will go on for the same reason the thirteen colonies took up arms against George III.

NEGRO MAN:

For like the colonies we have beseeched.

NEGRO WOMAN:

We have implored.

NEGRO MAN:

We have supplicated.

NEGRO MAN:

We have entreated.

NEGRO WOMAN:

We are writing our declaration of independence in shoe leather instead of ink.

WHITE MAN:

We're through with tokenism and gradualism and see-how-far-you've-comeism.

WHITE MAN:

We're through with we've-done-more-for-your-people-than-anyone-elseism.

NEGRO WOMAN:

We can't wait any longer.

NEGRO MAN:

Now is the time.

WHITE ACTOR (*stepping forward, reads from document*): We the people of the United States, in Order to form a more perfect Union . . .

WHITE ACTOR (*cont'd*): . . . establish Justice, insure domestic Tranquility, provide for the common defence, promote the general Welfare, and secure the Blessings of Liberty to ourselves and our Posterity, do ordain and establish this Constitution for the United States of America . . .

NEGRO ACTRESS (*sings under "We the people . . .," slowly building in volume*):

Oh, freedom—

Oh, freedom—

Oh, freedom over me!

And before I'll be a slave,

I'll be buried in my grave,

WHOLE CAST:
. . . And go home to my Lord
And be free!

Notes on the Documents

ACT I

1. The opening statements, meant to suggest the spectrum of current opinion, are taken from recent letters to the editors and articles in *Time, Newsweek, The New York Times,* and *The Atlanta Constitution.*

2. Falconbridge, Alexander, *Account of the Slave Trade on the Coast of Africa* (London: 1788).

The *Account,* a rare pamphlet, can be found more accessibly in George F. Dow, *Slave Ships and Slaving* (Salem: 1927), where it is reprinted on pp. 133–54.

The last sentence in this scene is out of sequence; I have taken it from an earlier section of the pamphlet.

3. *Annals of Congress,* Vol. I, pp. 1224–29.

The petition was not actually read to Congress by a Quaker woman, of course, but was introduced by a Representative. Also, the speeches themselves, which are here alternated between two actors, were in fact delivered by five separate Congressmen, and in different sequence from that presented in the scene.

4. The two opening sentences are from Jefferson's letter to Edward Coles, August 25, 1814; the remainder of the first paragraph is from Jefferson's *Autobiography* (1821). The rest of the speech is from his *Notes on Virginia* (1782). All are available in many editions: e.g., Adrienne Koch and William Peden, eds., *The Life and Se-*

lected Writings of Thomas Jefferson (New York: 1944), in which the selection from the Coles letter is on pp. 641–42, from the *Autobiography* on p. 51, and that from the *Notes on Virginia,* on pp. 257–62.

5. Olmsted, Frederick Law, *A Journey in the Seaboard States* (New York: 1856), pp. 676–84.

Olmsted's various travel accounts have been widely reprinted. The most comprehensive edition is Frederick Law Olmsted, *The Cotton Kingdom,* ed. Arthur M. Schlesinger. (New York: 1953), in which the material used for this scene can be found on pp. 259–65.

6. A Federal Writers' Project in the 1930's interviewed ex-slaves and recorded their reminiscences. These were deposited in the Library of Congress in over 10,000 manuscript pages. From these B. A. Botkin drew a representative sample which he published as *Lay My Burden Down* (Chicago: 1945)—now available in paperback. The material used in this scene can be found in the Botkin volume (in order of appearance) on pp. 125, 89, 123, 12, 84, 89–90, 25, 86, 122–23, 74, 73. In the second speech, I have combined reminiscences by two slaves into one narrative.

7. Jourdon Anderson's letter is in L. Maria Child, *The Freedmen's Book* (Boston: 1865), pp. 265–67; the Logue letters were printed in William Lloyd Garrison's newspaper, *The Liberator*, April 27, 1860. The Anderson letter has been reprinted more recently in *The Mind of the Negro as Reflected In Letters Written During the Crisis 1800–1860*, ed. Carter G. Woodson (Lancaster: 1926), pp. 537–39; and the Logue letters have been reprinted in Herbert Aptheker, *A Documentary History of the Negro People in the United States* (New York: 1951), pp. 449–51. The Aptheker volume is available in paperback.

8. *The Confessions of Nat Turner . . . ,* ed. Thomas R. Gray (Baltimore: 1831). This original edition is now rare; the *Confessions* is more readily available as reprinted in Aptheker, *op. cit.,* pp. 120–24.

9. May, Samuel J., *Some Recollections of Our Antislavery Conflict* (Boston: 1869), pp. 40–50, 71–72.

10. Sojourner Truth's speech was first printed in *History of Woman Suffrage*, Elizabeth Cady Stanton, Susan B. Anthony, and Matilda Joslyn Gage, eds. (New York: 1881), I, 116. More recently, it has been reprinted in *The Faith of Our Fathers*, Irving Mark and Eugene L. Schwaab, eds. (New York: 1952), pp. 33–34.

11. Sanborn, F. B., ed., *The Life and Letters of John Brown* (Boston: 1885). The speech to the court is printed on pp. 584–85; the final message to his guard, on p. 620.

12. Mary Boykin Chesnut, *A Diary from Dixie*, ed. Ben Ames Williams (Boston: 1949), pp. 31, 38, 292–93. The *Diary* is now available in a paperback edition.

13. Thomas Wentworth Higginson, *Army Life in a Black Regiment* (Boston: 1870), in order of appearance, pp. 7–8, 22–23, 53–54, 26, 76–77, 40–41. The volume is available in several paperback editions.

In selecting excerpts, I have not kept entirely to chronology; I have put Higginson's discussion of the soldiers' religion (in his diary, Jan. 13, 1863) before their prayers (in the diary, Dec. 14, 1862), and I have used the celebration of the Emancipation Proclamation (diary, Jan. 1, 1863), to close the scene.

ACT II

1. Recollections of the impact of freedom are in Botkin, *op. cit.*, in order of appearance, pp. 223, 66, 236–37, 225, 231, 267. The second speech, delivered by a woman, is actually the reminiscence of a man.

2. Elizabeth Hyde Bothume, *First Days Among the Contraband* (Boston: 1893), pp. 22, 35, 68. In a few places, I have changed tenses from past to present, and in the first paragraph, I have rearranged the sequence of sentences.

3. Eliza Andrews, *The Wartime Journal of a Georgia Girl* (New York: 1908), pp. 316, 365, 373–75.

4. The interview with President Johnson is printed in

Edward McPherson, *The Political History . . . of Reconstruction* (Washington: 1875), pp. 52–55.

After the Douglass delegation departed, Johnson, according to one of his private secretaries who was present at the interview, said: "Those d——d sons of b——s thought they had me in a trap! I know that d——d Douglass; he's just like any nigger, and he would sooner cut a white man's throat than not." (P. Ripley to Manton Marble, Feb. 8, 1866, Marble mss., as quoted in La-Wanda Cox and John H. Cox, *Politics, Principle, and Prejudice, 1865–1866* [Glencoe: 1963], p. 163).

5. The KKK oath and first testimony are from *Official Report of the Proceedings in the Ku Klux Trials . . . Before United States Circuit Court . . . Held at Columbia, South Carolina, November Term, 1871* (Columbia: 1872), p. 61 (the oath), p. 69 (testimony).

Mrs. Tutson's account is in *Testimony Taken by the Joint Select Committee to Inquire into the Conditions of Affairs in the Late Insurrectionary States* (Wash.: 1872), II, 59–64.

6. Senator Tillman's speech is in the *Congressional Record*, 59th Cong. 2d Sess., Vol. XLI, pp. 1440–44.

7. This famous "Atlanta Exposition" speech of Booker T. Washington's was widely quoted at the time (e.g. *The New York Times*, Sept. 19, 1895), and has since been widely reprinted. It may be conveniently found in Rayford W. Logan, *The Negro in the United States* (New York: 1957), pp. 128–30 (paperback).

8. W. E. B. DuBois "Of Mr. Booker T. Washington and Others," *The Souls of Black Folk* (Chicago: 1903), pp. 43–44, 50–51, 54–55. The volume is available in paperback.

9. This is Monroe Trotter's account of the interview with Wilson, as published in *The Crisis*, 9:119–27 (January 1915). It should not be assumed that because the version is Trotter's, it is necessarily unfair to Wilson; in fact it agrees, in broad outline, with all other accounts of the interview I have been able to find (e.g. *The New York Times*, Nov. 13, 1914). The Trotter version, however, is the only one I know which gives extensive dia-

logue exchange between the two men, and so the accuracy of the actual words spoken can not be entirely verified—an uncertainty which, though common to many (perhaps most) historical documents, makes this account something less than unimpeachable. Wilson's Secretary of the Navy, Josephus Daniels, visited Wilson the day after the Trotter interview, and later gave this account of the President's reaction:

"Daniels [Wilson said], never raise an incident into an issue. When the negro delegate threatened me, I was damn fool enough to lose my temper and to point them to the door. What I ought to have done would have been to have listened, restrained my resentment, and, when they had finished, to have said to them that, of course, their petition would receive consideration. They would then have withdrawn quietly and no more would have been heard about the matter. But I lost my temper and played the fool. I raised that incident into an issue that will be hard to down." (Daniels to Franklin D. Roosevelt, Mexico, June 10, 1933, Roosevelt Library, Official File 237. I am grateful to Arthur S. Link for this reference.)

The Trotter version occasionally switches from first person to third; wherever this happens, I have reconverted to first. The last line in the scene is a paraphrase taken from another account.

10. The French directive was originally discovered by W. E. B. DuBois on a trip to France following the Armistice. It was first printed in *The Crisis*, May 1919, pp. 16–18, and subsequently in Mary W. Ovington, *The Walls Came Tumbling Down* (New York: 1947), pp. 144–46. The directive was sent out at the request of the American Army by the French Committee, which was the official organ of communication between the American forces and the French. It represented American and not French opinion; when the French Ministry heard of the distribution of this document among the Prefects and Sous-Prefects of France, it apparently ordered copies of the directive to be collected and burned.

11. This composite speech of Marcus Garvey's is drawn from *The New York Times,* Aug. 3, 1920, and

The Independent, Feb. 26, 1921, pp. 205–6, 218–19.

12. The Father Divine letters were printed in his weekly newspaper, *The New Day,* June 9, 1951.

13. The laborer's description is from an account written early in the century (Hamilton Holt, ed., *The Life Stories of Undistinguished Americans as Told by Themselves* [New York: 1906], pp. 186, 190–92, 194, 198–99). Since peonage continued largely unchanged until at least World War II, I have felt at liberty to place this scene in the 1930's.

The storekeeper's speech is a paraphrase, with the names and amounts invented. In the last paragraph I have switched the sequence of three sentences.

14. Walter White's wartime experiences are in his autobiography, *A Man Called White* (New York: 1948), pp. 278–82, 285, 293.

15. The fifteen-year-old girl described her ordeal to Daisy Bates, president of the Arkansas N.A.A.C.P., who published the account in *Long Shadow of Little Rock* (New York: 1962), pp. 72–76. The white man's reaction, also as told to Mrs. Bates, is on pp. 69–71 of her book. I have put the two descriptions together into one scene.

16. The short closing statements are taken from recent letters to the editors and articles in *Time, Newsweek,* and *The New York Times.*

Appendix

ALTERNATE ENDING

The decision to make "Little Rock" the last major scene came about only after considerable experimentation. At various times later selections from Martin Luther King, James Baldwin, Malcolm X, and President Kennedy were added on, but I finally decided not to develop the post-1957 story fully; it was difficult to "top" the Little Rock scene dramatically, and, at any rate, I felt events since then were sufficiently familiar.

For the actual close of the play, I originally used a speech of Lincoln's instead of the Preamble to the Constitution. But this did not "play" as well as it read, and so the Preamble was substituted. As this is a reading version of the script, however, I thought it would be well to include the "Lincoln ending." Perhaps some future production might again wish to experiment with it as an alternate.

This speech would follow "*Now* is the time," and would be read instead of "We the people . . ." and without the singing of "Oh freedom. . .".

NEGRO ACTOR:

Fellow-citizens, *we* cannot escape history. We will be remembered in spite of ourselves. No personal significance, or insignificance, can spare one or another of us. The fiery trial through which we pass will light us down, in honor or dishonor, to the latest generation. We shall nobly save, or meanly lose, the last best hope of earth. The way is plain, peaceful, generous, just—a way which, if followed, the world will forever applaud, and God must forever bless. (*He closes book*)

Abraham Lincoln's second annual message to Congress. December 1, 1862.

Good night.

SAMPLE DOCUMENTS

These sample documents are published complete to give some idea of the editorial technique I used in preparing the script. The material in italics is that excerpted for a given scene. Any word which I have added or paraphrased is placed in brackets. Consult the notes for full source citations.

I. JEFFERSON ON THE NEGRO
(from his *Notes on Virginia*. This passage comes in a section dealing with revisions in Virginia's laws.)

The following are the most remarkable alterations proposed:

To emancipate all slaves born after passing the act. The bill reported by the revisors does not itself contain this proposition; but an amendment containing it was prepared, to be offered to the legislature whenever the bill should be taken up, and further directing that they should continue with their parents to a certain age, then be brought up, at the public expense, to tillage, arts or sciences, according to their geniusses, till the females should be eighteen, and the males twenty-one years of age, when they should be colonized to such place as the circumstances of the time should render most proper, sending them out with arms, implements of household and of the handicraft arts, seeds, pairs of the useful domestic animals & to declare them a free and independent people and extend to them our alliance and protection, till they shall have acquired strength; and to send vessels at the same time to other parts of the world for an equal number of white inhabitants; to induce whom to migrate hither, proper encouragements were to be proposed. It will probably be asked, Why not retain and incorporate the blacks into the State, and thus save the expense of supplying, by importation of white settlers, the vacancies they will leave? Deep rooted prejudices entertained by the whites; ten thousand recollections, by the blacks, of the injuries they have sustained; new provocations; the real distinctions which nature has made; and many other circumstances, will divide us into parties, and produce convulsions which will probably never end but in the extermination of the one or the other race.—To these objections which are political, may be added others which are physical and moral. The first difference which strikes us is that of colour. Whether the black of the negro resides in the reticular membrane between the skin and scarf skin, or in the scarf skin itself; whether it proceeds from the colour of the blood, the colour of the bile, or from that of some other secretion, the difference is fixed in nature, and is as real as if its seat and cause were better known to us. And is this difference of no importance? Is it not the foundation of a greater or less share of beauty in the two races? Are not the fine mixtures of red and white, the expressions of every passion by greater or less suffusions of colour in the one, preferable to that eternal monotony, which reigns in the countenances, that immoveable veil of black which covers all the emotions of the other race? Add to these, flowing hair, a more elegant symmetry of form, their own judgment in favour of the whites, declared by their preference of them as uniformly as is the preference of the Oran-ootan for the black women over those of his own species. The circumstance of superior beauty, is thought worthy attention in the propagation of our horses, dogs and other domestic animals; why not in that of man? Besides those of colour, figure, and hair, there are other physical distinctions proving a difference of race. They have less hair on the face and body. They secrete less by the kidnies, and more by the glands of the skin, which gives them a very strong and disagreeable odour. This greater degree of transpiration renders them more tolerant of heat, and less so of cold, than the whites. Perhaps too a difference of structure in the pulmonary apparatus, which a late ingenious * experimentalist has discovered to be the principal regulator of animal heat, may have disabled them from extricating, in the act of inspiration, so much of that fluid from the outer air, or obliged them in expiration, to part with more of it. They seem to require less sleep. A black, after hard labour through the day, will be induced by the slightest amusements to sit up till midnight or later, though knowing he must be out with the first dawn of the morning. They [*The blacks*] *are at least as brave, and more adventuresome. But this may perhaps proceed from a want of forethought, which prevents their seeing a danger till it be present.* When present, they do not go through it with more coolness or steadiness than the whites. *They are more ardent after their female: but love seems with them to be more an eager desire, than a tender delicate mixture of sentiment and sensation. Their griefs are transient. Those numberless afflictions which render it doubtful whether heaven has given life to us in mercy or in wrath, are less felt, and sooner forgotten with them. In general, their existence appears to participate more of sensation than reflection.* To this must be ascribed their disposition to sleep when abstracted from their diversions, and unemployed in labour. An animal whose body is at rest, and who does not reflect, must be disposed to sleep of course. Comparing them by their faculties of memory, reason and imagination, *it appears to me that in memory they are equal to the whites; in reason much inferior, as I think one could scarcely be found*

* Crawford.

capable of tracing and comprehending the investigations of Euclid: and that in imagination they are dull, tasteless, and anomalous. It would be unfair to follow them to Africa for this investigation. We will consider them here, on the same stage with the whites, and where the facts are not apocryphal on which a judgment is to be formed. *It will be right to make great allowances for the difference of condition, of education, of conversation, of the sphere in which they move.* Many millions of them have been brought to, and born in America. Most of them indeed have been confined to tillage, to their own homes, and their own society: yet many have been so situated that they might have availed themselves of the conversation of their masters; many have been brought up to the handicraft arts, and from that circumstance have always been associated with the whites. Some have been liberally educated, and all have lived in countries where the arts and sciences are cultivated to a considerable degree, and have had before their eyes samples of the best works from abroad. The Indians, with no advantages of this kind, will often carve figures on their pipes not destitute of design and merit. They will crayon out an animal, a plant, or a country, so as to prove the existence of a germ in their minds which only wants cultivation. They astonish you with strokes of the most sublime oratory; such as prove their reason and sentiment strong, their imagination glowing and elevated. But never yet could I find that a black had uttered a thought above the level of plain narration; never see even an elementary trait of painting or sculpture. In music they are more generally gifted than the whites with accurate ears for tune and time, and they have been found capable of imagining a small catch.* Whether they will be equal to the composition of a more extensive run of melody, or of complicated harmony, is yet to be proved. Misery is often the parent of the most affecting touches in poetry.—Among the blacks is misery enough, God knows, but no poetry. Love

---

* The instrument proper to them is the Banjar, which they brought hither from Africa, and which is the original of the guitar, its chords being precisely the four lower chords of the guitar.

is the peculiar oestrum of the poet. Their love is ardent
but it kindles the senses only, not the imagination. Religion indeed has produced a Phyllis Whately [1]; but
could not produce a poet. The compositions published
under her name are below the dignity of criticism. The
heroes of the Dunciad are to her, as Hercules to the
author of that poem. Ignatius Sancho [2] has approached
nearer to merit in composition yet his letters do more
honour to the heart than the head. They breathe the purest
effusions of friendship and general philanthropy, and
shew how great a degree of the latter may be compounded with strong religious zeal. He is often happy in the
turn of his compliments, and his stile is easy and familiar,
except when he affects a Shandean fabrication of words.
But his imagination is wild and extravagant, escapes incessantly from every restraint of reason and taste, and
in the course of its vagaries, leaves a tract of thought as
incoherent and eccentric as is the course of a meteor
through the sky. His subjects should often have led him
to a process of sober reasoning: yet we find him always
substituting sentiment for demonstration. Upon the whole,
though we admit him to the first place among those of
his own colour who have presented themselves to the public judgment, yet when we compare him with the writers
of the race among whom he lived, and particularly with
the epistolary class in which he has taken his own stand,
we are compelled to enroll him at the bottom of the
column. This criticism supposes the letters published under his name to be genuine, and to have received amendment from no other hand; points which would not be of
easy investigation. The improvement of the blacks in body
and mind, in the first instance of their mixture with the
whites, has been observed by every one, and proves that
their inferiority is not the effect merely of their condition
of life. [*Yet*] *We know that among the Romans*, about

---

[1] Phyllis Wheatley is the correct spelling. Her poems were published
in London in 1773. [M.B.D.]

[2] A resident of England, born a slave, Sancho's *Letters, with Memoirs of his Life*, appeared in 1782. [M.B.D.]

the Augustan age especially, *the condition of their slaves was much more deplorable than that of the blacks on the continent of America.* The two sexes were confined in separate apartments, because to raise a child cost the master more than to buy one. Cato, for a very restricted indulgence to his slaves in this particular, took from them a certain price. But in this country the slaves multiply as fast as the free inhabitants. Their situation and manners place the commerce between the two sexes almost without restraint.—The same Cato, on a principle of economy, always sold his sick and superannuated slaves. He gives it as a standing precept to a master visiting his farm, to sell his old oxen, old waggons, old tools, old and diseased servants, and every thing else become useless. 'Vendat boves vetulos, plaustrum vetus, ferramenta vetera, servum senem, servum morbosum, & si quid aliud supersit vendat.' Cato de re rusticâ. c. 2. The American slaves cannot enumerate this among the injuries and insults they receive. It was the common practice to expose in the island of Aesculapius, in the Tyber, diseased slaves whose cure was like to become tedious. The Emperor Claudius, by an edict, gave freedom to such of them as should recover, and first declared that if any person chose to kill rather than to expose them, it should be deemed homicide. The exposing them is a crime of which no instance has existed with us; and were it to be followed by death, it would be punished capitally. We are told of a certain Vedius Pollio who, in the presence of Augustus, would have given a slave as food to his fish, for having broken a glass. With the Romans, the regular method of taking the evidence of their slaves was under torture. Here it has been thought better never to resort to their evidence. When a master was murdered, all his slaves, in the same house, or within hearing, were condemned to death. Here punishment falls on the guilty one only, and as precise proof is required against him as against a freeman. Yet *notwithstanding* these and other discouraging circumstances among the Romans, *their slaves were often their rarest artists. They excelled too in science,* insomuch as to be usually employed as tutors to their master's children. Epictetus, Terence, and Phaedrus were slaves. *But they were of the race of whites.* It is not their condition then, but nature, which has produced the distinction.—Whether further observation will or will not verify the conjecture that nature has been less bountiful to them in the endowments of the head, I believe that in those of the heart she will be found to have done them justice. That disposition to theft with which they have been branded, must be ascribed to their situation, and not to any depravity of the moral sense. The man, in whose favour no laws of property exist, probably feels himself less bound to respect those made in favour of others. When arguing for ourselves, we lay it down as a fundamental that laws, to be just, must give a reciprocation of right: that, without this, they are merely arbitrary rules of conduct, founded in force, and not in conscience: and it is a problem which I give to the master to solve, whether the religious precepts against the violation of property were not framed for him as well as his slave? And whether the slave may not as justifiably take a little from one, who has taken all from him, as he may slay one who would slay him? That a change in the relations in which a man is placed should change his ideas of moral right and wrong, is neither new, nor peculiar to the colour of the blacks. Homer tells us it was so 2600 years ago

Ἥμισυ γάρ τ᾽ ἀρετῆς ἀποαίνυται εὐρύοπα Ζεύς
Ἀνέρος, εὖτ᾽ ἄν μιν κατὰ δούλιον ἦμαρ ἕλῃσιν. *Od. 17. 323.*

Jove fix'd it certain, that whatever day
Makes man a slave, takes half his worth away.

But the slaves of which Homer speaks were whites. Notwithstanding these considerations which must weaken their respect for the laws of property, we find among them numerous instances of the most rigid integrity, and as many as among their better instructed masters of benevolence, gratitude, and unshaken fidelity.—The opinion, that they are inferior in the faculties of reason and imagination, must be hazarded with great diffidence. *To justify a general conclusion, requires many observations,* even where the subject may be submitted to the Anatomical knife, to Optical glasses, to analysis by fire, or by solvents. How much more then where it is a faculty, not a substance we are examining; where it eludes the research of all the senses; where the conditions of its existence are various and variously combined; where the effects of those which are present or absent bid defiance to calculation; let me add too, as a circumstance of great tenderness, where our conclusion would degrade a whole race of men from the rank in the scale of beings which their Creator may perhaps have given them. To our reproach it must be said that, though for a century and a half we have had under our eyes the races of black and of red men, they have never yet been viewed by us as subjects of natural history. *I advance it therefore as a suspicion only, that the blacks, whether originally a distinct race, or made distinct by time and circumstances, are inferior to the whites in the endowments both of body and mind.* It is not against experience to suppose that different species of the same genus, or varieties of the same species, may possess different qualifications. Will not a lover of natural history then, one who views the gradations in all the races of animals with the eye of philosophy, excuse an effort to keep those in the department of man as distinct as nature has formed them? This unfortunate difference of colour, and perhaps of faculty, is a powerful obstacle to the emancipation of these people. Many of their advocates, while they wish to vindicate the liberty of human nature, are anxious also to preserve its dignity and beauty. Some of these, embarrassed by the question 'What further is to be done with them?' join themselves in opposition with those who are actuated by sordid avarice only. Among the Romans emancipation required but one effort. The slave, when made free, might mix with, without staining the blood of his master. But with us a second is necessary, unknown to history. When freed, he is to be removed beyond the reach of mixture . . .

II. LETTERS BETWEEN MRS. SARAH LOGUE AND HER EX SLAVE, REV. J. W. LOGUEN
(from *The Liberator,* April 27, 1860)

Maury County, State of Tennessee
Feb. 20, 1860.

TO JARM:—I now take my pen to write you a few lines, to let you know how we all are. I am a cripple, but I am still able to get about. The rest of the family are all well. Cherry is as well as common. *I write you these lines to let you know the situation we are in,—partly in consequence of your running away and stealing Old Rock, our fine mare. Though we got the mare back, she never was worth much after you took her;*—and, as I now stand in need of some funds, I have determined to sell you, and I have had an offer for you, but did not see fit to take it. *If you will send me one thousand dollars, and pay for the old mare, I will give up all claim I have to you.* Write to me as soon as you get these lines, and let me know if you will accept my proposition. *In consequence of your running away, we had to sell Abe and Ann and twelve acres of land; and I want you to send me the money, that I may be able to redeem the land* that you was the cause of our selling, and on receipt of the above-named sum of money, I will send you your bill of sale. *If you do not comply with my request, I will sell you to some one else, and you may rest assured that the time is not far distant when things will be changed with you.* Write to me as soon as you get these lines. Direct your letter to Bigbyville, Maury County, Tennessee. You had better comply with my request.

I understand that you are a preacher. As the Southern people are so bad, you had better come and preach to your old acquaintances. I would like to know if you read your Bible. If so, can you tell what will become of the thief if he does not repent? and, if the blind lead the blind, what will the consequence be? I deem it unnecessary to say much more at present. *A word to the wise is sufficient.* You know where the liar has his part. *You know that we reared you as we reared our own children;*

that you was never abused, and that shortly before you ran away, when your master asked you if you would like to be sold, you said you would not leave him to go with any body.

[*Yours, etc.*]
[*Mrs.*] *SARAH LOGUE.*

Syracuse, (N.Y.) March 28, 1860.

MRS. SARAH LOGUE: Yours of the 20th of February is duly received, and I thank you for it. It is a long time since I heard from my poor old mother, and I am glad to know that she is yet alive, and, as you say, "as well as common." What that means, I don't know. I wish you had said more about her.

You are a woman; but, *had you a woman's heart, you never could have* insulted a brother by telling him you *sold his [my] only remaining brother and sister, because he [I] put [my] himself beyond your power to convert him [me] into money.*

You sold my brother and sister, Abe and Ann, and twelve acres of land, you say, because I ran away. *Now you* have the unutterable meanness to *ask me to* return and be your miserable chattel, or, in lieu thereof, *send you $1000 to enable you to redeem the land, but not to redeem my poor brother and sister!* If I were to send you money, it would be to get my brother and sister, and not that you should get land. You say you are a CRIPPLE, and doubtless you say it to stir my pity, for you know I was susceptible in that direction. I do pity you from the bottom of my heart. Nevertheless, I am indignant beyond the power of words to express, that you should be so sunken and cruel as to tear the hearts I love so much all in pieces; that you should be willing to impale and crucify us all, out of compassion for your poor FOOT OR LEG. Wretched woman! Be it known to you that I value my freedom, to say nothing of my mother, brothers and sisters, more than your whole body; more, indeed, than my own life; more than all the lives of all the slaveholders and tyrants under heaven.

You say you have offers to buy me, and *that you shall sell me if I do not send you $1000, and in the same breath* and almost in the same sentence, *you say,* 'You know we *raised you as we did our own children.'* Woman, did you raise your own children for the market? Did you raise them for the whipping-post? Did you raise them to be driven off, bound to a coffle in chains? Where are my poor bleeding brothers and sisters? Can you tell? Who was it that sent them off into sugar and cotton fields, to be kicked and cuffed, and whipped, and to groan and die; and where no kin can hear their groans, or attend and sympathize at their dying bed, or follow in their funeral? Wretched woman! Do you say YOU did not do it? Then I reply, your husband did, and YOU approved the deed— and the very letter you sent me shows that your heart approves it all. Shame on you!

But, by the way, where is your husband? You don't speak of him. I infer, therefore, that he is dead; that he has gone to his great account, with all his sins against my poor family upon his head. Poor man! gone to meet the spirits of my poor, outraged and murdered people, in a world where Liberty and Justice are MASTERS.

But you say I am a thief, because I took the old mare along with me. Have you got to learn that I had a better right to the old mare, as you call her, than Mannasseth Logue had to me? Is it a greater sin for me to steal his horse, than it was for him to rob my mother's cradle, and steal me? If he and you infer that I forfeit all my rights to you, shall not I infer that you forfeit all your rights to me? Have you got to learn that human rights are mutual and reciprocal, and if you take my liberty and life, you forfeit your own liberty and life? Before God and high heaven, is there a law for one man which is not a law for every other man?

If you or any other speculator on my body and rights, wish to know how I regard my rights, they need but come here, and lay their hands on me to enslave me. *Did you think to terrify me by presenting the alternative to give my money to you, or give my body to slavery? Then let me say to you, that I meet the proposition with un-*utterable *scorn and contempt.* The proposition is an outrage and an insult. *I will not budge one hair's breadth. I will not breathe a shorter breath,* even to save me from your persecutions. *I stand among a free people,* who, I thank God, sympathize with my rights, and the rights of mankind; and if your emissaries and venders come here to re-enslave me, and escape the unshrinking vigor of my own right arm, I trust my strong and brave friends, in this city and State, will be rescuers and avengers.

Yours, etc.,
J. W. LOGUEN.

III. Senator Tillman on Lynching: The U.S. Senate, January 21, 1907
   (The earlier part of this speech, which is reprinted from the *Congressional Record,* Vol. XLI, deals with other matters.)

. . . the Senator from Wisconsin proceeded to quote from a former speech of mine in this body, in which I said:

We shot them; we killed them; and we will do it again.

When I asked for permission to point this out and show how unfair and unmanly was the attack he shut me off incontinently, refusing absolutely to give me an opportunity to explain or defend myself.

Now, what about those words of mine: "We shot them," etc. In what connection did I utter them? If I mistake not the Senator from Wisconsin was in this Chamber when I used that language. There were present a large number of leading Republicans. I challenged each and every man here to show wherein the people of South Carolina were not justified, and no one dared reply. I will repeat the statement of fact and circumstances. It was in 1876, thirty years ago, and the people of South Carolina had been living under negro rule for eight years. There was a condition bordering upon anarchy. Misrule, robbery, and murder were holding high carnival. The people's substance was being stolen, and there was no incentive to labor. Our legislature was composed of a majority of negroes, most of whom could neither read nor write. They were the easy dupes and tools of as dirty a band of vampires and robbers as ever preyed upon a prostrate people. There was riotous living in the statehouse and sessions of the legislature lasting from year to year.

Our lawmakers never adjourned. They were getting a per diem. They felt that they could increase their income by remaining in session all the while. They were taxing us to death and confiscating our property. We felt the very foundations of our civilization crumbling beneath our feet, that we were sure to be engulfed by the black flood of barbarians who were surrounding us and had been put over us by the Army under the reconstruction acts. The sun of hope had disappeared behind a cloud of gloom and despair, and a condition had arisen such as has never been the lot of white men at any time in the history of the world to endure. Life ceased to be worth having on the terms under which we were living, and in desperation we determined to take the government away from the negroes.

We reorganized the Democratic party with one plank, and only one plank, namely, that "this is a white man's country and white men must govern it." Under that banner we went to battle. We had 8,000 negro militia organized by carpetbaggers. The carpetbag governor had come to Washington and had persuaded General Grant to transcend his authority by issuing to the State its quota of arms under the militia appropriation for twenty years in advance, in order to get enough to equip these negro soldiers. They used to drum up and down the roads with their fifes and their gleaming bayonets, equipped with new Springfield rifles and dressed in the regulation uniform. It was lawful, I suppose, but these negro soldiers or this negro militia—for they were never soldiers—growing more and more bold, let drop talk among themselves where the white children might hear their purpose, and it came to our ears. This is what they said:

The President is our friend. The North is with us. We intend to kill all the white men, take the land, marry the white women, and then these white children will wait on us.

Those fellows forgot that there were in South Carolina some forty-odd thousand ex-Confederate soldiers, men who had worn the gray on a hundred battlefields; men who had charged breastworks defended by men in blue; men who had held lines of battle charged by men in blue; men who had seen real battles, where heroes fought. They forgot that putting in uniform a negro man with not sense enough to get out of a shower of rain did not make him a soldier. So when this condition of desperation had reached the unbearable point; when, as I say, despair had come upon us, we set to work to take the government away from them.

We knew—who knew better?—that the North then was a unit in its opposition to southern ideas, and that it was their purpose to perpetuate negro governments in those States where it could be done by reason of there being a negro majority. Having made up our minds, we set about it as practical men.

I do not say it in a boastful spirit, although I am proud to say it, that the people of South Carolina are the purest-blooded Americans in America. They are the descendants of the men who fought with Marion, with Sumter, with Pickens, and our other heroes in the Revolution. We have had no admixture of outsiders, except a small trickling in from the North and from other Southern States.

Clashes came. The negro militia grew unbearable and more and more insolent. I am not speaking of what I have read; I am speaking of what I know, of what I saw. There were two militia companies in my township and a regiment in my county. We had clashes with these negro militiamen. The Hamburg riot was one clash, in which seven negroes and one white man were killed. A month later we had the Ellenton riot, in which no one ever knew how many negroes were killed, but there were forty or fifty or a hundred. It was a fight between barbarism and civilization, between the African and the Caucasian, for mastery.

It was then that "we shot them;" it was then that "we killed them;" it was then that "we stuffed ballot boxes." After the troops came and told us, "You must stop this rioting," we had decided to take the government away from men so debased as were the negroes—I will not say baboons; I never have called them baboons; I believe they are men, but some of them are so near akin to the monkey that scientists are yet looking for the missing link. We saw the evil of giving the ballot to creatures of this kind, and saying that one vote shall count regardless of the man behind the vote and whether that vote would kill mine. So we thought we would let you see that it took something else besides having the shape of a man to make a man.

Grant sent troops to maintain the carpetbag government in power and to protect the negroes in the right to vote. He merely obeyed the law. I had no fault to find with him. It was his policy, as he announced, to enforce the law, because if it were bad then it would be repealed. Then it was that we stuffed ballot boxes, because desperate diseases require desperate remedies, and having resolved to take the State away, we hesitated at nothing.

It is undoubted that the Republicans will assume all responsibility for the condition in the South at that time. They have never shirked it. The Senator from Wisconsin acknowledged his participation in it the other day. He has no apology to make for it. I do not ask anybody to apologize for it; I am only justifying our own action. I want to say now that we have not shot any negroes in South Carolina on account of politics since 1876. We have not found it necessary. [Laughter.] Eighteen hundred and seventy-six happened to be the hundredth anniversary of the Declaration of Independence, and the action of the white men of South Carolina in taking the State away from the negroes we regard as a second declaration of independence by the Caucasian from African barbarism.

The other day the Senator from Wisconsin defined

liberty. "Liberty is that," I believe he said, "which is permitted by law to be done." The Senator has the right to give whatever idea of liberty he may have, and I have no objection to that. In a general way it is a very good definition. But I here declare that if the white men of South Carolina had been content to obey the laws which had been forced down our throats at the point of the bayonet and submit to the reconstruction acts which had thrust the ballot into the hands of ignorant and debased negroes, slaves five years before, and only two or three generations removed from the barbarians of Africa, the State of South Carolina to-day would be a howling wilderness, a second Santo Domingo. It took the State fifteen years to recover and begin to move forward again along the paths of development and progress; and in consequence of the white men interpreting the word "liberty" to mean the liberty of white people and not the license of black ones, the State is to-day in the very vanguard of southern progress, and can point to the result as the absolute justification for every act we performed in '76, however lawless our acts may be in the eyes of the Senator from Wisconsin.

South Carolina and Louisiana were the two last States to throw off the blood-sucking vampires which had been set over them by the reconstruction acts.

I would not have tried to do more than to give a statement of facts the other day, but I was not permitted to do so. I was ordered to take my own time, and I am now taking it in answer.

Now, *Mr. President, a word about lynching and my attitude toward it. A great deal has been said in the newspapers, North and South, about my responsibility in connection with this matter.* My position has been purposely misrepresented, and the Senator from Wisconsin has assumed to himself the right to arraign me in this body and to pass judgment of condemnation in most biting and vindictive phrase. It is not worth while to ask who made JOHN C. SPOONER my keeper or gave him the right to assume this hectoring and masterful attitude. With a self-righteousness that is characteristic of his breed, he dons the robe of the Pharisee, spreads broad his phylacteries, and calls up the Senator from South Carolina for sentence and pronounces his decree. These are his words:

MR. SPOONER. Now, Mr. President, I believe in law. I believe that wherever a man perpetrates a crime, or a crime is committed and the perpetrator or suspected perpetrator can be identified, the law should seize him. I believe he is entitled to a trial before sentence. I believe he is entitled to a day in court.

I am opposed, Mr. President, to any man making himself judge, juror, and executioner. I look upon it as shocking beyond expression in civilized communities, Mr. President, for the populace to seize a human being, charge him with crime, drag him to a tree protesting his innocence, and hang him or burn him at the stake. "In the corrupted currents of this world" it sometimes happens. All just men deplore it. No man ought to encourage it. It is a crime against civilization to encourage it.

I have looked with peculiar honor and pride upon the brave, continued efforts of southern governors to conserve the law, to maintain peace, to make that a real shield which the law in every civilized community is intended to throw around a man accused of crime. I have admired Governor Vardaman for it; I have admired the governors of other States in the South for it; I admire the governor anywhere who has done his uttermost to prevent lynching and to punish lynching.

And, Mr. President, I have been shocked more than once. I was shocked the other day here by the statement of the Senator from South Carolina justifying it and supporting its continuance. If there is one man under the sky who ought not to do it it is a maker of the laws which govern the people.

Mr. President, this is not an attack nor is it intended to be upon the Senator from South Carolina. It is a plea for good government, orderly government, real liberty—not the liberty of one man, but the liberty of all. What is liberty? It is not license. Liberty was once well defined to be "freedom to do that which the law permits." That is what liberty is. I say again that any man here or elsewhere who encourages lynching, murder, lawlessness, will have much to answer for, and the higher his position and the weightier his influence the more he will have to answer for.

Have I ever advocated lynch law at any time or at any place? I answer on my honor, "Never!" *I have justified it for one crime, and one only,* and I have consistently and persistently maintained that attitude for the last fourteen years. *As governor of South Carolina I proclaimed that, although I had taken the oath of office to support the law and enforce it, I would lead a mob to lynch any man,* black or white, *who had ravished a woman,* black or white. This is my attitude calmly and deliberately taken, and justified by my conscience in the sight of God.

Mr. President, the Senator from Wisconsin speaks of "lynching bees." As far as lynching for rape is concerned, the word is a misnomer. *When stern and sad-faced white men put to death a creature in human form who has deflowered a white woman,* there is nothing of the "bee" about it. There is more of the feeling of participating as mourner at a funeral. *They have avenged the greatest wrong, the blackest crime in all the category of crimes,* and they have done it, not so much as an act of retribution in behalf of the victim as a duty and as a warning as to what any man may expect who shall repeat the offense. They are looking to the protection of their own loved ones.

The Senator from Wisconsin prates about the law. He erects the law into a deity which must be worshiped regardless of justice. He has studied law books until his mind has become saturated with the bigotry which ignores the fundamental principle in this Government: "Law is nothing more than the will of the people." There are written laws and unwritten laws, and the unwritten laws are always the very embodiment of savage justice. The Senator from Wisconsin is incapable of understanding conditions in the South or else he has lost those natural impulses which for centuries have been the characteristics of the race to which we belong.

Tacitus tells us that the "Germanic people were ever

jealous of the virtue of their women." Germans, Saxons, Englishmen, they are practically one, springing from the same great root. That trinity of words, the noblest and holiest in our language, womanhood, wifehood, motherhood, have Saxon origin. I believe with Wordsworth—it is my religion—

A mother is a mother still, the noblest thing alive.

And a man who speaks with lightness or flippancy or discusses cold-bloodedly a matter so vital as the purity and chastity of womanhood is a disgrace to his own mother and unworthy the love of a good wife.

Look at our environment in the South, surrounded, and in a very large number of counties and in two States *outnumbered, by the negroes—engulfed, as it were, in a black flood of semi-barbarians.* Our farmers, living in segregated farmhouses, more or less thinly scattered through the country, have negroes on every hand. *For forty years these* [*negroes*] *have been taught the damnable heresy of equality with the white man,* made the puppet of scheming politicians, the instrument for the furtherance of political ambitions. Some of them have just enough education to be able to read, but not always to understand what they read. *Their minds are those of children, while they have the passions and strength of men.* Taught that they are oppressed, and with breasts pulsating with hatred of the whites, the younger generation of negro men are roaming over the land, passing back and forth without hindrance, and with no possibility of adequate police protection to the communities in which they are residing.

Now let me suppose a case. Let us take any Senator on this floor—I will not particularize—take him from some great and well-ordered State in the North, where there are possibly twenty thousand negroes, as there are in Wisconsin, with over two million whites. *Let us carry this* [*the*] *Senator* [*from Wisconsin*] *to the backwoods in South Carolina, put him on a farm miles from a town or railroad, and environed with negroes. We will suppose he has a fair young daughter just budding into womanhood; and recollect this, the white women of the South are in a state of siege;* the greatest care is exercised that they shall at all times where it is possible not be left alone or unprotected, but that can not always and in every instance be the case. *That Senator's daughter undertakes to visit a neighbor or is left home alone for a brief while. Some lurking demon who has watched for the opportunity seizes her; she is choked or beaten into insensibility and ravished, her body prostituted, her purity destroyed, her chastity taken from her, and a memory branded on her brain as with a red-hot iron to haunt her night and day as long as she lives.* Moore has drawn us the picture in most graphic language:

> One fatal remembrance, one sorrow that throws
> Its bleak shade alike o'er our joys and our woes.
> To which life nothing darker or brighter can bring,
> For which joy hath no balm and affliction no sting.

In other words, a death in life. This young girl thus blighted and brutalized drags herself to her father and tells him what has happened. Is there a man here with red blood in his veins who doubts what impulses the father would feel? Is it any wonder that the whole countryside rises as one man and with set, stern faces seek the brute who has wrought this infamy? Brute, did I say? Why, Mr. President, this crime is a slander on the brutes. No beast of the field forces his female. He waits invitation. It has been left for something in the shape of a man to do this terrible thing. *And shall such a creature, because he has the semblance of a man, appeal to the law? Shall men coldbloodedly stand up and demand for him the right to have a fair trial and be punished in the regular course of justice? So far as I am concerned he has put himself outside the pale of the law, human and divine. He has sinned against the Holy Ghost. He has invaded the holy of holies. He has struck civilization a blow, the most deadly and cruel that the imagination can conceive. It is idle to reason about it; it is idle to preach about it.*

Our brains reel under the staggering blow and hot blood surges to the heart. Civilization peels off us, any and all of us who are men, and we revert to the original savage type whose impulses under any and all *such circumstances has always been to "kill! kill! kill!"*

I do not know what the Senator from Wisconsin would do under these circumstances: neither do I care. I have three daughters, but, so help me God, I had rather find either one of them killed by a tiger or a bear and gather up her bones and bury them, conscious that she had died in the purity of her maidenhood, than have her crawl to me and tell me the horrid story that she had been robbed of the jewel of her womanhood by a black fiend. The wild beast would only obey the instinct of nature, and we would hunt him down and kill him just as soon as possible. What shall we do with a man who has outbruted the brute and committed an act which is more cruel than death? Try him? Drag the victim into court, for she alone can furnish legal evidence, and make her testify to the fearful ordeal through which she has passed, undergoing a second crucifixion?

Here is the picture drawn by a southern poet:

> A little woman, slight and deathly pale,
> Within her eyes
> The dim shame lingers of a sin unsinned.
> She speaks.
> Her voice is broken as her pride.
> It hath ·
> No music and no color and no warmth.
> From eyes like hers and tones like hers a man
> May learn how merciful is death.
> She tells
> The story of her guiltless infamy—
> Tells it beneath a fire of interruptions,
> Cross-questions, and objections, and the like,
> Sanctioned by Law's procedure.
> And insults from a shyster privileged
> Thro' his employment to insult her so—
> Tells it
> From start to finish, and is not spared a word,
> Until, at last,

A pitifully living corpse, she falls
Back into fearful silence.

*   *   *   *   *

And, facing her
The while, the Beast leans forward, huge and black,
Its simian arms crossed on the breast of it—
Whispering, at times, in the attorney's ears
Suggestions as to questions to be asked—
And tho' the fear of death and hell agape
Be in its belly, still unable quite
To hide a grin of reminiscent lust
Behind a sweating palm.

*   *   *   *   *

That is the picture—
Do I hear you say
Again: "The Law should take its course?"

— H. R. R. Hertzberg, New Orleans Harlequin.

That is what the Senator from Wisconsin says he would do, and he is welcome to all of the honor he can get out of it. Our rule is to make the woman witness, prosecutor, judge, and jury. I have known Judge Lynch's court to sit for a week while suspect after suspect has been run down and arrested, and in every instance they were brought into the presence of the victim, and when she said, "That is not the man," he was set free; but when she said, "That is the man," civilization asserted itself, and death, speedy and fearful, let me say—certainly speedy—was meted out. I have never advocated, I have deprecated and denounced, burning for this or any other crime. I believe it brutalizes any man who participates in a cruel punishment like that. I am satisfied to get out of the world such creatures.

[The speech goes on in a similar vein for many more pages. Below are a few of the noteworthy sections from the remainder of the speech.]

The Republican party itself has forsaken its old war cry of "the fatherhood of God and the brotherhood of man." It has denied the Filipinos any participation in the Government, proclaiming that they are not fit. The southern people know they are unfit. We do not dispute it; but in the name of common sense and honest dealing, if the Filipinos are unfit, why are the negroes fit? Everybody knows that the Caucasian stands first, the Mongolian second, the Malay third, the Indian fourth, and the negro fifth in the scale of civilization as fixed by ethnologists. We have had to deal with the other four races besides our own. We have excluded the Chinese. Why? In order to satisfy the selfish desire of white men who are interested. We have butchered the Indian and taken his land. We have settled him. We have denied that the Malay is fit. Yet here we stand proclaiming that the African is fit . . .

There was an irrepressible conflict in 1860 between slavery and freedom; between the idea of a confederation of States and a perpetual Union. Is there any man bold enough to deny that there is an irrepressible conflict now between civilization and barbarism and that the living together upon an absolute plane of equality of the two races in the South—one the highest, the other the lowest in the scale—is an impossibility without strife and bloodshed? . . .

The Senator from Wisconsin read the other day, with great pathos and effect, the eloquent speech of Henry Grady. There is not a line or a sentence in that noble deliverance to which I do not subscribe. The negroes whom Grady described were the negroes of the old slave days—the negroes with whom he played in childhood, the negroes with whom I played in childhood, the negroes who knew they were inferior and who never presumed to assert equality. For these negroes there is throughout the South a universal feeling of respect and love. I have not got it here, but I have at my home in the city a photograph of one of these. I might term him "Old Black Joe," for he is a full-blooded negro, about 60 years old. He has been living with me thirty-five years. He now has the keys to my home in South Carolina. He has full charge and control over my stock, my plantation. He is in every way a shining example of what the negro can be and how he can get along with the white man peacefully and pleasantly and honorably, enjoying all of his liberties and rights. But he has never meddled with voting. He occupies the same attitude as the white man and the negro do in this District. They do not meddle with voting. I do not hesitate to say, however, that a more loyal friend no man ever had. Every child that I have would share his last crust with that negro to-morrow . . .

Talk to me about hating these people! I do not do it. We took them as barbarians, fresh from Africa, the first generation we will say, or some of them twice removed, some of them once removed, some of them thrice removed, some of them a fourth removed from barbarism, but the bulk of them only twice. We taught them that there was a God. We gave them what little knowledge of civilization they have to-day. We taught them to tell the truth. We taught them not to steal. We gave them those characteristics which differentiate the barbarian and savage from the civilized man . . .

In 1865 the South, prostrate and bleeding and helpless, a very Niobe of nations, had the dead carcass of slavery chained to it by the fourteenth and fifteenth amendments. For eight years two States labored under it. One after another the others had thrown off for a little while the incubus—not getting loose, but simply getting relief, being able to stand up, to move, to breathe, and to make some progress. But there the carcass hangs, riveted to our civilization. The putrefaction is going on. A return to barbarism is evident in every day of our contact with these people in the South. Relieved from police control, they are no longer compelled, as the Indians have been by the troops, to stay on their reservations. These negroes move where they please. They have a little smattering of education. Some of them have white blood in their veins and taught that they are as good as the white man, they ask, Why not as good as a white woman? And when caste feeling and race pride and every instinct that influences and controls the white women makes them spurn the thought, rape follows. Murder and rape become a monomania. The negro becomes a fiend in human form . . .

[The speech ends as follows:]

As it is the South is helpless. We can do nothing. It is

not worth while for us to propose anything. All we can do is to maintain our present attitude of resistance, to maintain our control of our State governments, and to submit to whatever you see fit to do in national affairs, because under no conditions do we ever hope that the South can regain control of this Government. We are one-third of the population. You are two-thirds. Every year your numbers are being added to by a million immigrants in the North, who stay there, while none go to us. The million who came in last year represent five Congressmen. Those who came in year before last represent five more Congressmen. There is no danger of political power ever drifting away from the North as long as it maintains their superiority in population. No one expects to see that in this day or generation.

Therefore we say to you—I take the responsibility, if I am alone, of saying to you—it is your duty to do something. It is your duty to move. It is your duty to begin the discussion.

For the time being the South is occupying an attitude of waiting. It is occupying an attitude of constant friction, race riot, butchery, murder of whites by blacks and blacks by whites, the inevitable, irrepressible conflict between a white civilization and a black barbarism.

I plead for the negro as much as for the white man. This body of death is chained to our backs by two constitutional amendments, and I ask you in God's name, I ask you in the name of civilization, I ask you in the name of the virtue and purity of the white women of the South, to do something to relieve us from the body of this death. [Applause in the galleries.]

IV. A French Directive on the Treatment of Black
    American Troops
    (from *The Crisis*, May, 1919)

[*To the*] *French Military Mission stationed with the American Army. August 7, 1918. Secret information concerning the Black American Troops.*

It is important for French officers who have been

called upon to exercise command over black American troops, or to live in close contact with them, to have an exact idea of the position occupied by Negroes in the United States. The information set forth in the following communication ought to be given to these officers and it is to their interest to have these matters known and widely disseminated. It will devolve likewise on the French Military Authorities, through the medium of the Civil Authorities, to give information on this subject to the French population residing in the cantonments occupied by American colored troops.

1. The American attitude upon the Negro question may seem a matter for discussion to many French minds. But we French are not in our province if we undertake to discuss what some call "prejudice." *[recognize that] American opinion is unanimous on the "color question," and does not admit of any discussion.*

The increasing number of Negroes in the United States (about 15,000,000) would create for the white race in the Republic a menace of degeneracy were it not that an impassable gulf has been made between them.

As this danger does not exist for the French race, *the French public has become accustomed to treating the Negro with familiarity and indulgence.*

This indulgence and this familiarity *[These] are matters of grievous concern to the Americans. They consider them an affront to their national policy.* They are afraid that contact with the French will inspire in black Americans aspirations which to them (the whites) appear intolerable. *It is of the utmost importance that every effort be made to avoid profoundly estranging American opinion.*

Although a citizen of the United States, the black man is regarded by the white American as an inferior being with whom relations of business or service only are possible. The black is constantly being censured for his want of intelligence and discretion, his lack of civic and professional conscience, and for his tendency toward undue familiarity.

The vices of the Negro are a constant menace to the

American who has to repress them sternly. For instance, the black American troops in France have, by themselves, given rise to as many complaints for attempted rape as all the rest of the army. And yet the (black American) soldiers sent us have been the choicest with respect to physique and morals, for the number disqualified at the time of mobilization was enormous.

CONCLUSION

1. We must prevent the rise of any pronounced degree of intimacy between French officers and black officers. We may be courteous and amiable with these last, but we cannot deal with them on the same plane as with the white American officers without deeply wounding the latter. We *must not eat with* [*the blacks*] them, *must not shake hands or seek to talk or meet with them outside of the requirements of military service.*

2. We must not commend too highly the black American troops, particularly in the presence of (white) Americans. It is all right to recognize their good qualities and their services, but only in moderate terms strictly in keeping with the truth.

3. Make a point of keeping the native cantonment population from "spoiling" the Negroes. (White) *Americans become greatly incensed at any public expression of intimacy between white women with black men.* They have recently uttered violent protests against a picture in the "Vie Parisienne" entitled "The Child of the Desert" which shows a (white) woman in a "cabinet particulier" with a Negro. Familiarity on the part of white women with black men is furthermore a source of profound regret to our

experienced colonials who see in it an overweening menace to the prestige of the white race.

Military authority cannot intervene directly in this question, but it can through the civil authorities exercise some influence on the population.

[Signed] *Linard*

AFTERWORD: History and Theater*

Come, sit down, every mother's son, and rehearse your parts.—Shakespeare, *A Midsummer Night's Dream*

I suspect there are many besides myself who feel that historians are not communicating as well as they could, and that dramatists are not communicating as much as they might. It is the argument of this essay that the deficiencies of history and theater might be lessened if each would pay some attention to the virtues of the other.

First, however, I should make clear an underlying assumption: I believe the past has something to say to us. This may seem a truism, but an opposite view can be, and has been, cogently argued—the argument, if not the cogency, summed up in Henry Ford's statement, "History is all bunk." It is not my purpose to enter here in detail into the long-standing debate on whether history is or is not relevant to contemporary needs, can or cannot be objectively reconstructed, will or will not reflect the temporary bias of the historian and his culture. For the moment, I want only to make explicit my own premise that a knowledge of past experience can provide valuable guidelines, though not blueprints, for acting in the present. Those who do not share this assumption will hardly be concerned with the argument based upon it; there can be

* This essay was first printed, under the title "Presenting the Past," in the Fall, 1964, issue of *The Columbia University Forum* (Volume VII, Number 4). It has been partially revised by the author for this volume.

no wish to increase our awareness of the past if one holds that the past has no present meaning. And in the same way, those who believe that the theater is already rich enough in ideas and perspectives will have little patience with my further argument that its range needs amplification.

But to begin with history. Professional historians do, of course, worry about the shortcomings of their craft, but their dominant concern is with the difficulty of reconstructing past events "objectively." Handicapped both by the paucity of evidence and by the distortions in it which their own preconceptions introduce, historians have fits of self-doubt as to whether they are re-creating the past or merely projecting onto it their own, and their society's, transient needs. Yet few historians are concerned with shortcomings of another sort: whether their findings have much meaning for modern man. Too often today the academic historian seems to think his job is over once he has wrestled with the problems inherent in assembling data. He is, he would say, a scholar, not a policy adviser or a communications expert; it is up to others to draw and transmit the relevance of his findings.

Not only is the historian himself likely to be indifferent to the contemporary significance of his research, but suspicious of others who emphasize it; they are thought to be "propagandists." It is right, of course, to be on guard against any attempt to distort past evidence in the service of some present need. Yet such vigilance must be discriminating; a distinction should be made between reading contemporary meaning *into* the evidence, which is reprehensible, and reading it *from* the evidence, which is not. To do the latter is only to make explicit those conclusions already suggested by the data. The overt attempt to read "lessons" from history can, of course, be treacherous, but no worthwhile goal should be abandoned because it is difficult to attain. The effort to extract from the past something of use for our own experience is all that saves historical study from antiquarianism, the accumulation of detail for its own sake. If the past cannot be used—however conditionally—as a guide for the present, then its study is difficult to justify, at least to serious men. Historical writing becomes esthetics, the arrangement of past events in "pleasing" patterns, which, of course, can carry values of their own—except that historians have never been very good at esthetics. In asking them instead actively to search for "lessons," it should be stressed that no necessary threat is posed to historical objectivity. We would not ask historians to distort their findings, but to evaluate them, to be as eager to serve the living as the dead.

Assuming, then, that the past has some relevance for us, and that it is among a historian's proper functions —my own feeling is that it should be his preeminent function—to search for that relevance, it then becomes necessary to question the effectiveness with which such relevance (when found) is communicated. Since the invention of the printing press, the record of the past has been largely transmitted through the written word, and writing, a rational way of ordering and clarifying experience, makes an essentially intellectual appeal. Not always, of course, at the expense of the emotions: where the wish and skill are present, the writer can do much to evoke and engage our feelings. But the arousal of feelings is generally frowned on by the historian; emotion is thought to be an enemy rather than an adjunct of mind. Not surprisingly, therefore, historians have shown little regard for those literary skills best calculated to engage emotions. The majority of historians today eschew "lively" writing as a means of communication in much the same constricting way that they eschew relevance as its end. "Style" is thought to be an impediment to analysis, a frivolous sugar-coating repellent to those tough-minded heroes of the mind who prefer their ideas "straight."

Even were the historian more sensitive to the evocative potential of the written word, in immediacy he still could not rival the spoken word, which benefits from the direct confrontation of personality. In its beginnings, of course, the historical record *was* transmitted orally; in that sense, history began as theater. While no sensible person would advocate a return to this tradition, we may still wish to recapture something of its emotional impact. If we could bring the spoken word's immediacy and emotion to the presentation of history, a new richness of response, a new measure of involvement with the past, would be possible.

Almost all combinations of history and theater have been made by dramatists, with the result—as in Shakespear's *Richard II* or John Osborne's *Luther*—that historical episodes have been used, shaped, and embellished for imaginative purposes. The past event becomes the occasion for a statement not in itself strictly historical. This is in accord with a writer's usual procedure; he transposes the raw material of experience, he makes it his own and, if he has sufficient insight and artistry, everyone's.

But the imaginative reworking of historical data is fundamentally inimical to what the professionals regard as "proper" history. The historian knows that his personality influences his interpretations, but this is not the same, he would say, as advocating such influence; a virtue should not be made of necessity. Control and restriction of interaction between the subjective historian and his "objective" materials is essential. This intellectual fastidiousness may severely limit the opportunity for speculation, but it also minimizes the risk of contaminating the data. The professionals, in short, prefer to emphasize information rather than informing.

Yet the contrast between the historian's "objective" presentation of the past and, say, the novelist's subjective reworking of it, is overdrawn. It describes the historian's intention more than his result, for in a real sense he too necessarily indulges in imaginative combinations of fact and opinion. Historical writing is never merely litmus paper, recording an exact facsimile of past events, but always consists to some degree of one man's idiosyncratic interaction with the data. It may be, too, that if the historian is ever to make widely relevant statements, he will have to become more consciously and extensively the philosopher *commenting* upon historical materials.

But if the contrast between the writing of history and fiction has been overdrawn, it is nevertheless a contrast the historian cherishes. He would protest being asked to play philosopher speculating on human ends, or psychologist investigating human needs, or novelist describing human conditions. He defines the role of a historian as simply one of collecting and recording what survives of past experience, *not* commenting upon it. Given this self-image, he objects especially to the "distortions" which a writer like John Osborne makes in the historical record when converting it for the stage. This, the historian would say, is adding immediacy and emotion to the past at the sacrifice of accuracy and intellectual subtlety.

An historian myself, I am sympathetic to these professional scruples even while not being fully convinced by them. Despite the risks, it seems to me worth searching for valid ways to combine history and theater, and not only to enrich historical presentation, but also to revitalize theatrical statement. For the benefits of a union between history and drama would not by any means be all on one side. If theater, with its ample skill in communication, could increase the immediacy of past experience, history, with its ample material on human behavior, could broaden the range of theatrical testimony. And there are grounds for believing that the theater's present range is badly in need of amplification.

The current mode of dramatic writing has been variously called the theater of the absurd, the theater of revolt, the theater of despair. The ugly, the empty, the irrational, the mechanical, the brutal, the apathetic—these are the dominant themes of contemporary theater. And they may well be the dominant themes of contemporary life. Perhaps today's playwrights, whose personal lives, we are told, have often been so melancholy, overdo the importance of these themes, confusing their own sorrows with the world's decline. But if the modern playwright has overdrawn the disintegrative aspects of modern life, it is not by much, judging from what we see around us. And the evidence of our senses is corroborated by the evidence of science. The portrayal of human behavior in the theater of the absurd closely resembles the description provided by sociologists, psychologists, and anthropologists. Man, these behavioral scientists tell us, *is* a creature who flees reality, who prefers comfortable deceptions to hard truths, whose yearning for approval drives him to think and act as his society dictates, whose libidinous instincts can propel him into brutal, selfish, destructive behavior. Thus the behavioral view of man seems to support the current theatrical view of man. If, therefore, we take the function of drama to be the accurate reflecting of contemporary life, the state of our current theater must be judged satisfactory. Or, if unsatisfactory, only because our playwrights have not described the modern predicament with sufficient skill; the failure, according to this canon, would be one of execution, not intent.

It is possible to suggest, though, that the intent as well is too restricted. There is no inherent reason why drama need be limited to describing what *is*; it could also become concerned with what *might be*. One function of the theater should obviously be to reflect the actuality of life, but another might be to change it. Instead, by presenting man largely as brute, child or fool, the current theater fortifies and perpetrates those qualities. If men are told that they are at the mercy of impulse and irrationality, they become more likely to behave accordingly. Like it or not, the theater, partaking as it does of self-fulfilling prophecy, is a social force, though at present an inadvertent and negative one. Man's destructive qualities are real enough and must be faced. But other qualities—or at least potentials—are real as well, and they too should be brought to attention. At present they are not. Theater audiences see little to counteract the view that self-deception, hysteria, and savagery are synonyms for human nature.

Once again, the perspective of behavioral science is useful. Just as its findings validate the theater of the absurd, so they also support the need to supplement it. Psychologists and sociologists have made abundantly clear the immense plasticity and enormous adaptive power of human beings; if social demands and emphases are shifted, human action shifts accordingly. Thus, if we would not today celebrate man's innate goodness, we should be equally ready to recognize that nothing predetermines him to be cruel, vacuous, and selfish. As Berelson and Steiner point out in *Human Behavior*, man's "evil comes from frustration, not from inherent nature . . . he seeks acceptance . . . more than he seeks political power or economic riches, and he can even control his strongest instincts, the libidinous side of his nature, to this end." Man is not only a social creature, but also a social product. If challenged to do so, he is capable of using reason and will to develop integrative, and control destructive, impulses. Why should not the theater put such a challenge to him? Why could it not help to alter the destructive behavioral patterns it now merely describes? There is no inherent reason why drama cannot be an agency of amelioration as well as a voice of despair.

We need not be sentimental about all this and emblazon Victorian mottoes like SHINE IN USE on our playbills. I am certainly not suggesting that the theater of absurdity be supplemented by some crude theater of "positive thinking." I am suggesting only that since integrative experiences exist in our lives, they should also have some representation in our theater. Though despair and disintegration may well characterize the dominant mood today, they do not tell the whole story either of our present condition, or, more significantly still, of our potential one. The theater, by making room for a demonstration of other aspects of human nature, could help to see that the current mood of disintegration does not become the permanent one.

One way (though certainly not the only one) of demonstrating man's potential for a wide variety of experiences and behavior, is to put more history on the stage, either in fictional or documentary form. Both approaches have their drawbacks. Those characterizing fiction, (à la Osborne), have already been discussed; my own experience with the documentary approach may serve to illustrate the special problems of that form.

In wanting to tell the story of being black "in white America" with maximum impact, I thought it worth trying to combine the evocative power of the spoken word with the confirming power of historical fact. Yet I did not wish to sacrifice historical accuracy in the process. And so I tried staging the raw material of history itself rather than a fictionalized version of it. The two modes of procedure, of course, are not entirely different—as I argued earlier. Using historical documents—letters, news reports, diaries, and the like—does not guarantee objectivity; it would be naïve to think that in selecting, abridging, cutting, and juxtaposing the materials of history, I was not also transmuting them. The past does not speak for itself, and the ordering intelligence that renders it, necessarily injects some degree of idiosyncrasy. The advantage of the documentary approach (if one is primarily interested in historical accuracy) is that it does at least minimize subjectivity and restrict invention. Its disadvantage (if one is primarily interested in making statements about experience) is that it circumscribes reflection and generalization. Instead of confining myself, for example, to the actual words John Brown spoke at his trial, I might have invented words to represent what I guessed to be his thoughts and feelings during his speech. In not doing so, I suspect that what I gained in accuracy I lost in insight. Truth of fact has less durable relevance than truth of feeling, for a fact is rooted in a particular context, whereas a feeling, being universal, can cross time.

There are, then, inherent difficulties in putting history on the stage: fictionalization can caricature the past, documentation can straitjacket it. Yet both techniques seem worth experimenting with, for history and theater, though the union be flawed, can contribute much to each other.

The great virtue of history, one the theater stands in need of, is that it counteracts present-mindedness—the belief that what *is* has always been and must always be. To have historical perspective is to become aware of the range of human adaptability and purpose. Thus the ancient world (and the eighteenth-century Enlightenment) saw man as a creature capable of using reason to perceive and follow "virtue"; the Christian view saw man capable of love as well as sin; the Renaissance believed that man's energy and will were sufficient to control both his personal destiny and his social environment.

Such views, of course, were philosophical models of what men could be, not necessarily what they were. But the dominant outlook of any period reflects actual as well as ideal behavior, for men build their self-images out of their experience as well as their aspirations. At any period, to be sure, ideal behavior is only approximated. Enlightenment France may have believed in the possibility —and necessity—of a rational life, but it was hardly free of sophistry and corruption; moderns have neither invented nor discovered man's capacity for the irrational and the vicious. But in other eras such qualities were not considered sufficient descriptions of human nature or insurmountable barriers to human aspiration; men could, they were told, resist their destructive impulses, could lead more than merely instinctive lives.

No doubt most of us today proceed on similar assumptions in daily life. But the assumptions get less formal recognition than they once did. We are not encouraged —in our culture generally, in our theater particularly— to recognize that human nature is malleable, capable of many forms and many goals. We are not encouraged to see that "absurdity" is only a partially true description of the way we live, and even more, that it tells us little of how we *might* live.

It is not the responsibility of the Albees or the Becketts to show us what we might be; their responsibility is to their own, not to all possible, visions. But for those concerned with the future as well as the present, something more in our theater wants saying. To recognize that human beings are curious, do strive, will reason, can love, is to wish for a theater that might express and encourage this kind of human potential—precisely because that potential is scarcely visible today. We need the theater of the absurd to dramatize our weaknesses and failings, but we also need theater which might indicate our potential strengths and possible successes.

Putting history on the stage is hardly a cure-all. Not only does the technique, as I have argued, hold intrinsic difficulties, but it is true as well that historical theater would not necessarily be a theater of "affirmation"; undoubtedly much in man's past experience would underscore, rather than counteract, present pessimism. My only point is that the totality of past experience does include more than despair and defeat; there *is* material in history which chronicles achievement and possibility. Such evidence is around us today as well, of course, but we seem unable to use it; it may be a case of not being able to see the forest for the trees. This is exactly why an historical context may be needed if the "positive" aspects of human experience are to become accessible.

Merging the competencies of history and drama, therefore, could help to diminish the parochialism of both. Currently, historical study is fixated on past patterns and the theater on present ones; neither is sufficiently concerned with the future. If the variety of past experience could be communicated with an immediacy drawn from the theatrical idiom, both history and drama might become vehicles for change rather than only the recorders, respectively, of past and present attitudes. In being more fully exposed to the *diversity* of past human behavior, we might come to see that men (even if only *sometimes*) can give purpose and structure to their lives; can use the tensions of existence creatively, or at the worst, accept them with dignity; can, without sacrificing self-interest, treat others with respect and compassion. Such an awareness could be a useful corrective to the current penchant for underestimating ourselves, which, after all, is but one way of excusing and indulging our defeats.

                                        MARTIN B. DUBERMAN

Plays by Tennessee Williams

☐ **CAT ON A HOT TIN ROOF.** A drama of the seething passions that beset a Southern family in a shattering moment of revelation. (#T3547—75¢)

☐ **THE NIGHT OF THE IGUANA.** The emotion-charged story about two women who vie for the affections of a defrocked minister. The movie starred Richard Burton, Ava Gardner, Deborah Kerr, and Sue Lyon.
(#P3244—60¢)

☐ **PERIOD OF ADJUSTMENT.** A Broadway comedy that explores the exasperating personality conflicts in two shaky marriages. (#D2210—50¢)

☐ **A STREETCAR NAMED DESIRE.** The Pulitzer Prize-winning play of a woman betrayed by love.
(#P2924—60¢)

☐ **SUDDENLY LAST SUMMER.** The compelling play about a corrupt sensualist and a beautiful girl.
(#P3326—60¢)

☐ **SWEET BIRD OF YOUTH.** The story of an aging actress and her protege and lover. (#P2856—60¢)

SIGNET Pla...

☐ **THE AME**... ...**RY by Ed-**
ward Albe... ...Broadway
plays by ... ...ay, **Who's**
Afraid of ... ...92—60¢)

☐ **THE SANDBOX AND THE DEATH OF BESSIE SMITH by**
Edward Albee. Two plays—a scathing domestic tragedy,
and an explosive drama baring the ugly circumstances
surrounding the death of a great Negro blues singer.
(#P2339—60¢)

☐ **LUTHER by John Osborne.** A brilliant play about the
rebellious priest who challenged and changed the spir-
itual world of his time. By the author of **Look Back in**
Anger.   (#Q3677—95¢)

☐ **BECKET by Jean Anouilh.** The compelling drama of
Thomas à Becket, Archbishop of Canterbury, and of
King Henry II of England, explores the changing relation-
ship between two men bound for separate destinies. The
movie starred Richard Burton and Peter O'Toole.
(#P2453—60¢)

☐ **A RAISIN IN THE SUN by Lorraine Hansberry.** The
Broadway hit about a young Negro father desperately
trying to break free from the barriers of prejudice.
(#P2642—60¢)

☐ **SUNRISE AT CAMPOBELLO by Dore Schary.** The superb
drama about Franklin D. Roosevelt, how he was stricken
by polio, and emerged triumphant from his ordeal.
(#T3515—75¢)

THE NEW AMERICAN LIBRARY, INC., P.O. Box 2310, Grand Central
Station, New York, New York 10017

Please send me the SIGNET BOOKS I have checked above. I am
enclosing $_____(check or money order—no currency
or C.O.D.'s). Please include the list price plus 10¢ a copy to cover
mailing costs. (New York City residents add 5% Sales Tax. Other
New York State residents add 2% plus any local sales or use taxes.)

Name_____

Address_____

City_____State_____Zip Code_____
Allow at least 3 weeks for delivery